The Rise of Political Islam in Turkey

Angel Rabasa • F. Stephen Larrabee

Prepared for the Office of the Secretary of Defense

NATIONAL DEFENSE RESEARCH INSTITUTE

This research was sponsored by the Under Secretary of Defense for Policy and was conducted within the International Security and Defense Policy Center of the RAND National Defense Research Institute, a federally funded research and development center sponsored by the Office of the Secretary of Defense, the Joint Staff, the Unified Combatant Commands, the Department of the Navy, the Marine Corps, the defense agencies, and the Defense Intelligence Community under contract W74V8H-06-C-0002.

Library of Congress Cataloging-in-Publication Data

Rabasa, Angel.
    The rise of political Islam in Turkey / Angel Rabasa, F. Stephen Larabee.
      p. cm.
    Includes bibliographical references.
    ISBN 978-0-8330-4457-0 (pbk. : alk. paper)
    1. Islam and politics—Turkey. 2. Islam and state—Turkey. 3. Islam—Turkey—History. I. Larabee, F. Stephen. II. Title.

BP63.T8R33 2008
322'.109561—dc22

                                                        2008009764

The RAND Corporation is a nonprofit research organization providing objective analysis and effective solutions that address the challenges facing the public and private sectors around the world. RAND's publications do not necessarily reflect the opinions of its research clients and sponsors.

RAND® is a registered trademark.

Cover design by Rod Sato

Published 2008 by the RAND Corporation
1776 Main Street, P.O. Box 2138, Santa Monica, CA 90407-2138
1200 South Hayes Street, Arlington, VA 22202-5050
4570 Fifth Avenue, Suite 600, Pittsburgh, PA 15213-2665
RAND URL: http://www.rand.org/
To order RAND documents or to obtain additional information, contact Distribution Services: Telephone: (310) 451-7002;
Fax: (310) 451-6915; Email: order@rand.org

Preface

Turkey is a Muslim-majority country that is also a secular democratic state, a member of NATO, a candidate for membership in the European Union, a long-standing U.S. ally, and the host of İncirlik Air Base, a key hub for logistical support missions in Afghanistan and Iraq. As such, Turkey is pivotal to U.S. and Western security interests in a critical and unstable zone where the Middle East, the Balkans, and the Caucasus intersect. Turkey's importance derives not only from its geopolitical position, but also from the example that it provides of the coexistence of Islam with secular democracy, globalization, and modernity. Of course, the Turkish experiment with the rule of a party with Islamic roots, the Justice and Development Party (AKP), within a framework of strict secularism has generated controversies over the boundaries between secularity and religion in the public sphere—tensions that were brought to a head over the selection of the new president and that led to parliamentary elections, along with a new mandate for the party, in July 2007.

This monograph describes the politico-religious landscape in Turkey and the relationship between the state and religion, and it evaluates how the balance between secular and religious forces—and between the Kemalist elites and new emerging social groups—has changed over the past decade, particularly since the AKP came to power in 2002. The study also assesses the new challenges and opportunities for U.S. policy in the changed Turkish political environment and identifies specific actions that the United States may undertake to advance the U.S. interest in a stable, democratic, and friendly Turkey and, more broadly, in the worldwide dissemination of liberal and pluralistic interpretations of Islam.

The analytical framework for this study follows that of recent RAND work on politico-religious trends in the Muslim world, particularly *The Muslim World After 9/11*, by Angel Rabasa, Cheryl Benard, Peter Chalk, C. Christine Fair, Theodore W. Karasik, Rollie Lal, Ian O. Lesser, and David E. Thaler (MG-246-AF, 2004). This research was sponsored by the Under Secretary of Defense for Policy and was conducted within the International Security and Defense Policy Center of the RAND National Defense Research Institute, a federally funded research and development center sponsored by the Office of the Secretary of Defense, the Joint Staff, the Unified Combatant Commands, the Department of the Navy, the Marine Corps, the defense agencies, and the Defense Intelligence Community.

The authors can be contacted by e-mail at rabasa@rand.org or larrabee@rand.org; by phone at 703-413-1100, ext. 5268 or 5218; or by mail at The RAND Corporation, 1200 South Hayes Street, Arlington, VA 22202-5050.

For more information on RAND's International Security and Defense Policy Center, contact the Director, James Dobbins. He can be reached by email at James_Dobbins@rand.org; by phone at 703-413-1100, ext. 5134; or by mail at The RAND Corporation, 1200 S. Hayes Street, Arlington, VA 22202-5050. More information about RAND is available at www.rand.org.

Contents

Figures and Table

Figures

Table

Summary

As a Muslim-majority country that is also a secular democratic state, a member of NATO, and a long-standing U.S. ally, Turkey is pivotal to U.S. strategy to shape the Middle Eastern security environment. Turkey is also a key test case for the role of Islam in politics and its influence on external policy. Until recently, Islamic parties in Turkey were largely a fringe movement. However, the success of the Justice and Development Party (AKP) in the past two national elections demonstrates the growing strength of a political movement with Islamic roots. That said, the AKP does not define itself as an Islamic party, and its electoral success does not translate into popular support for an Islamist agenda. Although the AKP won an overwhelming victory in the July 2007 election, it still faces serious challenges, including the possibility that it could be closed down.

While the AKP has Islamist roots, it is fundamentally different from its predecessors—the National Salvation, Welfare, and Virtue parties—in terms of its ideology, its political goals, its market-oriented economic program, and the broader range of the electorate to which it appeals. Despite its origins, the AKP government has not pursued an overt Islamist agenda (although critics accuse it of seeking to infiltrate Islamists into the civil bureaucracy and condoning Islamization at the local level). The AKP government has given priority to pursuing Turkey's European Union (EU) membership, economic stabilization, and reform of the legal system over divisive symbolic issues such as the Islamic headscarf controversy. Secularists, however, worry about "creeping Islamization."

Alternative Political Futures

How deep-seated Turkey's (and the AKP's) transformation is and the impact it will have on Turkey's future political development and foreign policy orientation remain open questions. In the aftermath of the July 2007 elections, the AKP has substantially strengthened its hold on power. A senior party member, former Foreign Minister Abdullah Gül, has been elected president, fundamentally altering the previous political landscape in which a secularist president counterbalanced the AKP-dominated parliament. The party's future remains uncertain, as a result of the indictment forwarded to the Constitutional Court in March 2008 calling for the closing of the party for violating the principles of secularism.

Over the next decade, Turkey could evolve in a number of different ways. Four possible "alternative futures" for Turkey are described below. Some are more likely than others, but all are plausible enough that they deserve serious consideration and analysis.

Scenario 1: The AKP Pursues a Moderate, EU-Oriented Path

In this scenario, the AKP solidifies its hold on power and maintains a moderate path, not allowing Islamist impulses in its foreign policy to derail its EU-oriented course. Some erosion of the restrictions on public expressions of religiosity occurs, and individuals are given greater latitude to express a more visible Islamic identity. However, no attempt is made to introduce Islamic legislation, such as Islamic legal codes. At the same time, efforts are made to reduce the political role of the military. The AKP government also seeks to loosen restrictions on religious minorities.

Until early 2008, this seemed to be the most likely scenario. However, the indictment of the AKP forwarded by the Public Prosecutor to the Constitutional Court has called this assumption into question. If, in the end, the AKP is not closed and remains in power, it is likely to be more cautious about pressing for measures that could be perceived as changing the secular-religious balance or provoking the secularists into another attempt to remove it from power. The presence of AKP members and religious-school graduates in the government bureaucracy is

likely to continue to expand. At the local level, some AKP-run municipal councils are likely to continue efforts to infuse their conception of
Islamic morality into public policy.

There are, however, structural limits on how far a reelected AKP
government can go in opening space for Islam in the public sphere.
The Kemalist establishment remains largely intact. Any government
that crosses the lines that define the acceptable role of religion in politics risks accentuating political tensions and possibly provoking intervention by the military. In addition to the political constraints posed
on the AKP's freedom of action by the military and secular elements
in the bureaucracy, the judiciary, and the higher educational establishment, two other factors argue for a moderate course by an AKP
government.

One is the moderate and pluralistic tradition of Islam (discussed
in the chapter on the Islamic landscape in Turkey). Rigid Salafi interpretations of Islam have never taken root within a broad sector of the
Turkish population. Public-opinion polls show that there is little support in Turkey for an Islamic state.[1] A large majority of Turks, including religious Turks, support the secular state.

The other factor arguing for a moderate course is that Turkey is
imbedded in the West, institutionally, economically, strategically, and,
to a significant degree, culturally as well. Over the past two decades,
Turkey has converged significantly with European norms. Important
gaps remain, but the trends are clear. The implication of this is that
Islamic politics in Turkey are affected more by the international context than is generally the case in the Middle East.

Although these considerations argue for a moderate trajectory for
religious politics in a democratic and increasingly globalized Turkey,
other, less positive outcomes are possible. Three possible alternatives
are described below.

---

[1] For instance, a poll by the highly respected Turkish Economic and Social Studies Foundation (TESEV) published in 2006 found that only 9 percent of the Turkish population
favored a state based on the *shari'a* (down from 21 percent in 1999). See Ali Çarkoğlu and
Binnaz Toprak, *Değişen Türkiye'de Din Toplum Ve Siyaset*, Istanbul: TESEV, 2006, p. 11.

Scenario 2: Creeping Islamization

In this scenario, the reelected AKP government pursues a more aggressive Islamist agenda. With full control of the executive and legislative branches of government, the AKP is able to appoint administrators, judges, and university rectors and even to influence personnel decisions in the military. In foreign policy, the AKP intensifies ties to the Muslim world, especially to Iran and Syria. Faced with growing opposition in Europe to its bid for EU membership, the AKP turns to an effort to create a competing Islamic bloc.

"Creeping Islamization" is the scenario that worries most secularists, many of whom fear that the AKP harbors a hidden agenda to Islamize Turkish society. However, in our view, this scenario is less likely, for several reasons. First, it would lead to greater political polarization and would likely provoke intervention by the military. Second, most Turks support a secular state and oppose a state based on the *shari'a*. Third, EU membership has been a core element of the AKP's foreign policy. While discontent with the EU has been increasing, EU membership is still supported by more than half of the Turkish population.

Scenario 3: Judicial Closing of the AKP

In this scenario, the Constitutional Court closes down the AKP. Closing down the AKP, however, would solve little and could lead to a deepening of the crisis. As its strong showing in the July 2007 elections underscores, the AKP enjoys broad political support throughout the country. If it is closed, the party is likely to simply reemerge under another name—as happened when the MSP (National Salvation Party) and the RP (Welfare Party) were banned. Closing the AKP would also increase strains with the EU and further complicate Turkey's quest for EU membership.

Scenario 4: Military Intervention

A fourth possibility is an escalation of social tensions that leads to intervention by the military. A confrontation could take place if the AKP takes actions seen by the military as crossing important lines. The military-intervention scenario has two possible variants: (1) a "soft coup," where the military mobilizes social pressure against the AKP, eventually forcing it to resign, and (2) a direct military intervention leading to the forcible removal of the AKP government and the disbanding of the party. While direct intervention by the military cannot be excluded from consideration, especially if the AKP begins to push an Islamic agenda more aggressively, it is not very likely and would occur only as a last resort after the military had exhausted all other options.

Implications for U.S. Policy

The examination of Islam's role in Turkey leads to several conclusions and implications for U.S. policy.

The first relates to the nature of Islam in Turkey and its role in Turkish political life. Turkey has a long history, dating back to the late Ottoman period, of seeking to fuse Islam and Westernization. This differentiates Turkey from other Muslim countries in the Middle East and enhances the chances that it will be able to avoid the sharp dichotomies, ruptures, and violence that have characterized the process of political modernization in the area.

This is important, because it goes to the heart of the issue of the compatibility of Islam and democracy. The ability of a party with Islamic roots to operate within the framework of a secular democratic system while respecting the boundaries between religion and state would refute the argument that Islam cannot be reconciled with modern secular democracy. On the other hand, if the experiment fails, it could lead to greater secular-Islamic polarization, further reducing the middle ground needed to build the moderate Muslim bulwark needed to contain the spread of radicalized Islam.

Beyond Turkey, the accommodation of Islam with democracy and secularism that has been achieved there is a valuable resource in the current ideological conflict between radical and mainstream interpretations of Islam. Mainstream entities in Turkey, therefore, should be encouraged to partner with groups and institutions elsewhere in the Muslim world to propagate moderate and pluralistic interpretations of Islam.

U.S. policymakers should be cautious, however, about portraying Turkey as a "model" for the Middle East. That notion makes many Turks, especially the secularists and the military, uncomfortable, because they believe that it pushes Turkey politically closer to the Middle East and weakens Turkey's Western identity. In addition, they fear that it will strengthen political Islam in Turkey and erode the principle of secularism over the long run.

A second conclusion relates to the sources of Turkey's transformation. The growing strength of political Islam in Turkey (or rather, of politics informed by Islam) has been largely a response to internal factors, particularly the democratization and socioeconomic transformation of Turkish society over the past several decades. An important corollary to this point is that the United States may not have much leverage in this sphere. It also highlights the importance of cultivating new and diverse elites.

Third, it is an oversimplification to see the current political tensions in Turkey as a struggle between "Islamists" and "secularists." Rather, these tensions are part of a struggle for power between newly emerging social sectors and the secularized elite—a struggle between the "periphery" and the "center"—that has deep roots in Ottoman and recent Turkish history. The democratization of Turkish society since the mid-1980s has opened up political space for forces that had been largely excluded from politics (including Islamists) to organize and propagate their views.

Fourth, while the AKP has Islamic roots, it enjoys broad-based political support that transcends religious, class, and regional differences. Its widespread social networks and efficient party machine, with close ties to local constituencies, have enabled it to gain strong support among the poor and marginalized groups that make up a growing portion of Turkey's urban areas. At the same time, its liberal, free-market economic policies attract the provincial entrepreneurial classes that are socially conservative but integrated into the global economy. The AKP's support for democratic reform and its tolerant policy toward minorities have also enabled it to obtain the support of many members of minority communities.

Fifth, in the past decade, the AKP has undergone an ideological transformation, abandoning the anti-Western rhetoric that characterized its Islamist predecessors and embracing a new discourse that emphasizes values consistent with those of Western societies. This shift is most visible in the AKP's position on Turkish membership in the EU. The shift has resulted in an important realignment in Turkish politics. In the past, the Kemalists were the main proponents of close ties to the West and Western integration. In recent years, however, this role has increasingly been assumed by the AKP. Ironically, as the AKP has pressed forward with reforms designed to bring Turkey into conformity with EU norms and regulations, some sectors in the Kemalist establishment and the military have begun to worry that EU membership and further democratization could undermine Turkish security, as well as their own political role.

Turkey's prospects for attaining EU membership remain uncertain. While the EU Commission supports continuing accession negotiations, opposition in Europe to Turkish membership is growing—on cultural as well as political grounds. Although the United States is not a member of the EU, it has a stake in how the membership issue is managed. Turkey's integration into the EU would strengthen the EU, as well as Turkey's Western orientation, and would rebut the claim that the West—especially Europe—is innately hostile to Muslims. On the other hand, rejection of Turkey's candidacy could provoke an anti-Western backlash, strengthening those forces in Turkey that want to weaken Turkey's ties to the West.

Sixth, Turkish policy toward the Middle East is likely to remain a sensitive issue in bilateral U.S.-Turkish relations. Turkey's growing interests in the Middle East are likely to make Ankara wary about allowing the United States to use its military facilities for regional contingencies except where such operations are clearly perceived to be in Turkey's interest. This argues for a diversification of U.S. access options that would provide alternatives to Incirlik Air Base in case Turkey increases restrictions on U.S. use of it or other Turkish facilities.

The Armenian genocide resolutions periodically introduced in the U.S. Congress could also cause strains in relations with Ankara in the future. In 2007, the Bush administration succeeded in getting a genocide resolution (HR-106) shelved at the last second, narrowly averting a serious crisis with Ankara. However, the resolution is likely to be reintroduced and to remain a potential source of discord. Future administrations will need to work closely with congressional leaders to ensure that the Armenian issue does not poison future relations with Turkey.

The United States also needs to deal more resolutely with the terrorist attacks against Turkish territory by the Kurdistan Workers' Party (PKK). In Turkish eyes, the PKK issue is the litmus test of the value of the U.S.-Turkish security relationship. How the United States responds to this issue will have a seminal influence on the tenor of U.S.-Turkish relations over the next decade.

The closer military and intelligence cooperation with Ankara against the PKK since Prime Minister Recep Tayyip Erdoğan's visit to Washington in November 2007 has helped to defuse some of the mistrust and tension in bilateral relations that has built up since—and, to a large degree, as a consequence of—the Iraq war. But it needs to be followed up by other concrete steps. In particular, the United States should put greater pressure on the Kurdistan regional government to crack down on the PKK and cease its logistical and political support of the group. At the same time, while a tough anti-terrorist program is an important component of a strategy to defeat the PKK, it must be combined with social and economic reforms that address the root causes of the Kurdish grievances.

Acknowledgments

The authors wish to thank all those who made this study possible. First of all, we wish to acknowledge the invaluable contributions of our reviewers, Ian Lesser, Senior Transatlantic Fellow, The German Marhall Fund of the United States; and Soli Özel, Professor of Political Science at Bilgi University. We also thank Emre Erkut, a key member of our research team who is currently a doctoral fellow at the Frederick S. Pardee RAND Graduate School. It goes without saying that we are entirely responsible for any errors that remain.

Our most important sources of information were Turkish government officials, academics, and members of civil society, including, among the latter, representatives of the Alevi, Jewish, Greek, and Armenian communities. For their cooperation in this project, we wish to thank in particular Sabit Şimşek, Director of the Inter-Religious Dialogue Branch of the Presidency of Religious Affairs of Turkey; Şerif Mardin for his important insights into Turkish history; Can Paker, Chairman of the Board of the Turkish Economic and Social Studies Foundation (TESEV); Ali Çarkoğlu of Sabanci University; Nilüfer Narlı of Bahçeşehir University; Hüseyin Özcan of Fatih University; Ömer Bolar, Yusuf Cevahir, and Hakan Kıyıcı of the Independent Industrialists and Businessmen's Association (MÜSİAD); Cemal Uşak, Harun Tokak, and the staff of the Journalists and Writers Foundation (GYV); Yusuf Kanlı, Editor-in-Chief, and Mustafa Akyol, Deputy Editor, of *Turkish Daily News*; Ekrem Dumanlı, CEO and Editor-in-Chief, and Abdülhamit Bilici, Deputy Editor-in-Chief, of *Zaman*; Mehmet Ali Birand, member of the Executive Committee of *CNN Turk*; Cengiz

Çandar, journalist, *Referans;* and Egemen Bağiş, Reha Çamuroğlu, and Suat Kınıklıoğlu, members of the Turkish parliament, AKP.

We also thank The Honorable Ross Wilson, U.S. Ambassador to Turkey. In the United States, we thank General (retired) Joseph Ralston, Vice Chairman, The Cohen Group; Michael Rubin of the American Enterprise Institute; and Hasan Ali Yurtsever of the Rumi Forum in Washington, D.C., for his assistance in establishing contact with religious organizations in Turkey.

Within RAND, the authors wish to thank Ambassador (retired) James Dobbins, Director, Center for International Security and Defense Policy, for his support for this project; Nathan Chandler for his technical assistance; our editor Janet DeLand; our production editor Josh Levine; and Mary Wrazen, who designed the cover of the report.

Acronyms and Abbreviations

AKP	Justice and Development Party (*Adalet ve Kalkınma Partisi*)
ANAP	Motherland Party (*Anavatan Partisi*)
CHP	Republican People's Party (*Cumhuriyet Halk Partisi*)
DFD	Lighthouse Charitable Association (*Deniz Feneri Derneği*)
DP	Democratic Party
DTP	Democratic Society Party (*Demokratik Toplum Partisi*)
DYP	True Path Party (*Doğru Yol Partisi*)
FP	Virtue Party (*Fazilet Partisi*)
GYV	Journalists and Writers Foundation (*Gazeteciler ve Yazarlar Vakfı*)
IGMG	*Islamische Gemeinschaft Millî Görüs*
MGK	National Security Council (*Milli Güvenlik Kurulu*)
MNP	National Order Party (*Milli Nizam Partisi*)
MSP	National Salvation Party (*Milli Selamet Partisi*)
MÜSİAD	Independent Industrialists' and Businessmen's Association (*Müstakil Sanayici ve Işadamları Derneği*)
PKK	Kurdistan Workers' Party (*Partiya Karkerên Kurdistan*)
RP	Welfare Party (*Refah Partisi*)

SP	Felicity Party *(Saadet Partisi)*
TESEV	Turkish Economic and Social Studies Foundation *(Türkiye Ekonomik ve Sosyal Etüdler Vakfı)*
TGS	Turkish General Staff
TRT	Turkish Radio and Television Corporation
TÜSİAD	Turkish Industrialists' and Businessmen's Association *(Türk Sanayicileri ve İşadamları Derneği)*
YÖK	Higher Education Council *(Yüksek Öretim Kurulu)*

CHAPTER ONE

Introduction

Politics and Religion in Turkey

As a Muslim-majority country that is also a secular democratic state, a member of NATO, and a long-standing U.S. ally, Turkey is pivotal to U.S. strategy for shaping the Middle Eastern security environment. However, Turkey has not been immune to the changes that have transformed the religiopolitical landscape of the Muslim world in recent decades, which include an increase of religiosity and an upsurge in the political expression of Islam. These trends were generated by a variety of factors, including the emergence of a religious entrepreneurial sector and of a dominant political party with Islamic roots, a more open debate about Kemalism and its relevance to contemporary Turkish society, and a political crisis over the selection of a new president in the spring and summer of 2007.

Contemporary Turkey is a key test case for the role of Islam in politics and its influence on external policy. It is also a distinctive, possibly unique, case in several respects. The Justice and Development Party (*Adalet ve Kalkınma Partisi* (AKP)), led by Recep Tayyip Erdoğan, rules as a solid majority government, having trounced all rivals in Turkey's November 2002 elections and further reinforced its position with strong results in 2004 local elections. The AKP won an impressive 46.6 percent of the vote in the July 2007 election—increasing its electoral vote by 12 percent over its performance in 2002—although because of the mathematics of the distribution of seats in parliament, the number of seats held by the AKP decreased from 362 to 340, short of the two-thirds needed to amend the constitution.[1]

Even before the AKP's victory in the 2002 general elections, there was a substantial religious component in Turkish politics. The dominant center-right parties of the 1980s and early 1990s, the True Path Party (*Doğru Yol Partisi* (DYP)) and the Motherland Party (*Anavatan Partisi* (ANAP)), always contained significant socially conservative wings. Necmettin Erbakan founded a series of Islamist parties over the past 30 years and was very influential as deputy prime minister in the 1970s and briefly as prime minister in the 1990s. Before the advent of multiparty democracy in the 1950s, Islamism had no expression in the political system, which was the exclusive domain of the official Kemalist party, the Republican People's Party (CHP).

Despite its Islamist roots, the AKP government has not pursued an overt Islamist agenda (although critics accuse it of seeking to infiltrate Islamists into the civil bureaucracy and condoning Islamization at the local level). The Erdoğan government has given priority to pursuing Turkey's EU membership, economic stabilization, and reform of the legal system. These reforms have included the abolition of the death penalty, "civilianization" of the National Security Council, broadcasting in Kurdish by the state-owned Turkish Radio and Television Corporation (TRT), and ratification of international human rights conventions.[2] The Erdoğan government has been less aggressive than many had hoped it would be in reforming or scrapping the controversial Article 301 of the Turkish constitution, which criminalizes insults to "Turkishness." Opposition from nationalists and Kemalists, as well as the presence of conservative nationalists within its own ranks, along with the rising mood of nationalism, leave the AKP little room for maneuver in this area.

---

[1] The Turkish electoral system sets a 10 percent threshold for a political party's representation in parliament; in 2002, only one other party, the *Cumhuriyet Halk Partisi* (CHP), passed the threshold, disproportionately increasing the number of AKP seats. In 2007, a third party, the *Milliyetçi Hareket Partisi* (MHP), also passed the threshold, bringing about an overall reduction in the number of seats held by the AKP and the CHP.

[2] İhsan Dağı, "Turkish Politics at the Crossroads," presentation at the German Marshall Fund of the United States conference, Washington, D.C., February 8, 2007.

Yet there continues to be an active debate over the real nature of the AKP's agenda and close scrutiny of its credentials as a self-proclaimed "conservative democratic party." Erdoğan professes to lead a movement of "Muslim Democrats"—rather like Christian Democrats in Western Europe—in which religion is a cultural backdrop rather than an active part of the political agenda. Opinions are divided on whether this approach represents a genuine expression of a new synthesis in Turkish politics or a tactic to hold Turkey's entrenched secularists, including the military (and constitutional strictures against religious politics), at bay.

Elements within the AKP, and in the religious parties to the right of it, would surely like to press a more Islamic social agenda. Pragmatists within the party, including Erdoğan and President Abdullah Gül, recognize the risks of doing so. Against this background, the selection of Gül as president and possible constitutional changes proposed by the AKP will be key tests of the secular-religious balance in the country.

Turkey's "recessed" Islamic politics—with religion as an implicit rather than an explicit part of political discourse—is one source of Turkish distinctiveness.[3] This is a function of Turkey's form of secularism: based on the French model of *laïcité*, but with state-religion relations rooted in the Ottoman tradition that subordinates religion to state authority. Turkey's constitution places firm limits on expressions of political Islam. Religious associations—Sufi orders, for instance—cannot operate legally.

To be sure, Turkish secularism in the Kemalist mold is evolving under the pressure of a more cosmopolitan intellectual debate. The private practice of religion is more widely accepted today, even within secular circles. Secularists certainly want to limit the role of religion in Turkish politics, but the automatic association of religiosity with a backward, Middle Eastern outlook is now less common. The common denominator of Turkish secularists is, above all, a desire to prevent the erosion of their highly Westernized way of life. Much of the sec-

---

[3] See Ian O. Lesser, "Turkey: 'Recessed' Islamic Politics and Convergence with the West," in Rabasa et al., *The Muslim World After 9/11*, Santa Monica, CA: RAND Corporation, MG-246-AF, 2004.

ular urban middle class views the implications of Islamist influence through a "lifestyle" lens. Concerns about political Islam per se or a strategic drift to the "East" are more prevalent among intellectuals, business elites, and the secular political class.

Another source of Turkey's distinctiveness is history, what the distinguished Turkish scholar Şerif Mardin calls "Turkish exceptionalism."[4] The Ottoman Empire was the seat of the caliphate and thus the center of Muslim political power and presence in international relations into the early years of the 20th century. Atatürk's secular revolution modernized and Westernized Turkey in key respects. But even after 85 years, the results of this experiment are contested. Turkey remains a place of sharp regional, class, and cultural differences, and these unresolved tensions are part of the contemporary Turkish political landscape. The AKP's success can be explained in large measure by the way in which the movement has captured a sense of Turkish popular dissatisfaction with established political elites. A key question is whether the AKP will maintain its present course, or whether the crumbling of institutional restraints or pressures from more-radical elements will lead it to embrace a more overtly religious agenda.

A key factor shaping Turkey's evolution is the EU accession process, even if many in Europe are trying to keep Turkey at arms' length. The EU project represents a convergence of the AKP's international and domestic strategic goals. The AKP discovered human rights and democracy as a means of protecting itself from authoritarian Kemalists. It realized the advantages of speaking the language of democracy—which enables the party to communicate with the West and to reassure those who suspect that it may secretly harbor an Islamist agenda. Erdoğan has spoken about "marketing Turkey" and has defended the idea of globalization. The West, in turn, has emerged as an ally of the AKP.[5]

---

[4] Şerif Mardin, "Turkish Islamic Exceptionalism Yesterday and Today," *Journal of International Affairs,* Vol. 54, No. 1, Fall 2000, pp. 146–147.

[5] Dağı, op. cit.

Structure of the Report

This report explores the ways in which the political balance in Turkey between secular and religious forces, and within Turkish Islamic movements and organizations, has changed since the election of the AKP government, and it assesses challenges and opportunities for U.S. policy in the changed Turkish political environment. Chapter Two discusses Turkey's Islamic landscape, including the origins, development, and distinctive features of Islam in Turkey. Chapter Three explores the domestic and international factors that contributed to the development of political Islam in Turkey and, specifically, to the rise of the AKP, while Chapter Four examines the AKP's record in power and its relationship with the military and with non-Muslim minorities. Chapter Five examines the Erdoğan government's foreign policy. Finally, Chapter Six derives overall observations and conclusions and the implications of these developments for U.S. policy toward Turkey.

CHAPTER TWO

The Islamic Landscape in Turkey

Turkey has a complex and extraordinarily rich religious tradition, ranging from pre-Islamic practices to mainstream Sunni Islam, from small minority groups of Orthodox Christians, as well as Jews, to a range of Alevis, Shi'a, and other sects. Turkey is, of course, an overwhelmingly Muslim society, but 80 years of a rigorously secular republic have placed religion in the realm of private practice for most Turks. The emergence of a more visible "religiosity" on the Turkish scene, especially over the past decade, is a product of many influences: the waning of the Kemalist legacy, a rediscovery of traditional practices, an expanding network of religious schools and social-welfare institutions, and the process of democratization and the rise of a more openly religious middle class. It is also the visible product of large-scale migration from the countryside to the cities in recent decades, with a consequent movement of more-traditional, more outwardly religious people to Turkey's modern, urbanized west.[1]

The role of Islam in Turkish political leadership was a contested issue even in the Selçuk and Ottoman periods. Thus, the more direct confrontation between Islam and secularism in republican Turkey has historical roots.[2] From the late 17th century onward, with the erosion

---

[1] This chapter builds on Ian O. Lesser, "Turkey: 'Recessed' Islamic Politics and Convergence with the West," op. cit.

[2] See Bernard Lewis, *The Emergence of Modern Turkey*, London: Oxford University Press, 1975; and Lord Kinross, *The Ottoman Centuries: The Rise and Fall of the Turkish Empire*, New York: Morrow Quill, 1977.

of the power of the sultan, the religious leadership (the *ulema*) became steadily more influential, and high-ranking mufti became central actors in Ottoman politics and foreign affairs.[3] The balance of political and religious authority shifted again in the later years of the Ottoman Empire, as restive Arab populations outside Anatolia came to see the caliphate as part of a Turkish colonial empire, and as the Ottoman regime and liberal reformers pushed the country toward modernization, Western practices, and de facto secularization.[4]

Atatürk's abolition of the caliphate in 1924 and the enactment of a series of sweeping secularization measures greatly reinforced a trend toward secularization that had much earlier roots but remains a contested issue in Turkish society. Analysts of political Islam in Turkey often cite the general subordination of religious to political authority in Ottoman and post-Ottoman Turkey as an argument against the potential for the emergence of a religious state in modern Turkey.[5]

In recent decades, reformist thinking has been gaining ground among Turkish theologians. There is an argument that the globalization and modernization of Turkish society have produced a demand for modern Islam. Beginning with the Nur movement, religious schools of thought have emerged that do not see conflict between reason and revelation and have internalized concepts of political democracy, religious toleration, rule of law, and a free-market economy. This, too, makes Turkey different from the other countries of the Middle East, where modernist interpretations of Islam have found it difficult to make inroads against entrenched religious conservatism.

---

[3] Doğu Ergil, *Secularism in Turkey: Past and Present*, Ankara: Turkish Foreign Policy Institute, 1995, pp. 4–5. Others have suggested that the effective embodiment of the religious establishment's role in the state was the office of Şeyhülislam, or chief mufti. See Binnaz Toprak, *Islam and Political Development in Turkey*, Leiden, The Netherlands: E. J. Brill, 1981, pp. 30–43.

[4] Ergil, op. cit., p. 5.

[5] See comments by Soner Cagaptay and others, cited in Jean-Christophe Peuch, "Turkey: What Remains of Political Islam?" Radio Free Europe/Radio Liberty, at www.Rferl.org/features/2003/01/10012003163109.asp (as of March 21, 2008).

Religion, Ethnicity, and Politics

Religion and politics in Turkey are influenced by the country's ethnic and demographic situation. Throughout the Ottoman period, until as late as the 1920s, the state was a diverse patchwork of ethnic and religious communities. In the first parliament of the Ottoman Empire, which convened in 1877 during the reign of Abdulhamit II, the elected lower house (*Meclis-i Mebusan* (Assembly of Representatives)) consisted of 69 Muslims and 46 non-Muslims.[6] By this measure, modern republican Turkey is actually more homogeneous and less cosmopolitan than its imperial predecessor. Orthodox Christians, Jews, and other non-Muslims are dwindling minorities in today's Turkey. That said, the secular nature of the republic offers the remnants of these once very large communities a relatively stable, if sometimes uneasy, environment.

The continuing potential of minority issues to serve as flashpoints for religious and nationalist sentiment was dramatically underscored by the 2007 murder in Istanbul of Hrant Dink, a prominent Turkish-Armenian journalist and intellectual. The murder spurred an outpouring of sentiment by moderate Turks, deeply troubled by an example of what many see as rising intolerance and xenophobia in Turkey (trends witnessed in parts of Europe as well). The daily newspaper *Vatan* reported that "it has been alleged that the aggressor shouted, 'I killed an Armenian,' when running away from the attack scene."[7] In response, 5,000 demonstrators marched from Taksim Square to the murder scene and shouted, "We are all Hrant Dinks, we are all Armenians."[8]

---

[6] The upper house (*Meclis-i Ayan* (Assembly of Elites)) was composed of 26 members selected by the sultan. The breakdown of the upper house's composition is not available. İlk Parlamento, Geçmişten Günümüze TBMM, Türkiye Büyük Millet Meclisi, at http://www.tbmm.gov.tr/tarihce/kb2.htm (as of March 21, 2008).

[7] "Türkiye'ye daha büyük kötülük yapılamazdı," *Vatan,* January 20, 2007.

[8] "Hepimiz Ermeniyiz," *Hürriyet,* January 20, 2007. The killer's social environment and link to the nationalist network have subsequently been uncovered, and it is clear that the murder was motivated by nationalism, not religion. Although there are reports that the killer shouted, "I killed a non-Muslim," the possible Turkish words for that (*gayrimüslim* or *gavur*) are also routinely used to mean "non-Turkish minority" or simply "minority." In common Turkish parlance, minority refers to Armenians, Greeks, and Jews only.

Although ethnic Turks constitute a majority of the country's population, Turkey remains an ethnically diverse society. Kurds represent about one-fifth of the population, and the issue of Kurdish integration remains the leading internal social—and security—issue facing the country. Kurds predominate in southeast Anatolia, with large communities outside Turkey in northern Iraq, Iran, and Syria. Yet a majority of Turkey's Kurds now live outside their traditional areas, as the result of large-scale migration to urbanized western Turkey in recent decades. This pattern of demographic change has been reinforced by the strains of a 15-year insurgency and counterinsurgency in the Kurdish areas of the southeast.

Beyond ethnic identification, many Turks can and do trace their origins to areas outside Anatolia, whether in the Caucasus, the Balkans, Central Asia, or elsewhere in the Levant. These affiliations have come to play a more prominent role in Turkish politics and foreign policy in recent decades and have become the basis for lobbies on Chechnya, Bosnia, Azerbaijan, and the status of the Turkomen in Iraq. Kemalist ideology, apart from being vigorously secular, left little room for these ethnic identifications. For Atatürk, the Turkish identity was a question of location rather than ethnicity: Turks were those living within Turkey who called themselves Turks. But in popular perception, the line between Turkish nationalism and ethnic and religious identity has often been blurred.

Ethnicity, regionalism, and religious politics interact in several ways in contemporary Turkey. More traditional and visible Islamic practices are common in rural and poorer areas of the country, particularly in the southeast.[9] Migration to the cities has changed the composition of the urban areas in the west, which now include large areas inhabited by poor, more-traditional, and more-religious populations. Religious parties have done well in the southeast and among migrants to the cities, often outcompeting Kurdish nationalist parties. This was certainly a factor in the electoral success of the Islamist Refah Party in

---

[9] For an analysis of the urban-rural dimension in the resurgence of Turkish religiosity, see Nur Vergin, "De-Ruralization in Turkey and the Quest for Islamic Recognition," *Private View* (Istanbul), Vol. 1, No. 1, Winter 1996, pp. 50–54.

1995, when the party garnered 21.5 percent of the vote and led a coalition, as well as its successor, *Fazilet* (Virtue Party), and more recently, the AKP. The more-radical currents in Islamic politics such as Turkish Hezballah are also more visible in the urban areas of southeastern and eastern Anatolia, where it is often alleged that such groups were supported by Ankara as part of the counterinsurgency strategy against the Kurdistan Workers Party (PKK) in the 1990s.

The PKK and other Kurdish separatist movements have, in general, been oriented toward the secular left, rather than the Islamic right. Religious extremism among Turkey's Kurds has never been a comfortable fit with Kurdish nationalism. At another level, however, the perception of disenfranchisement and alienation among many Kurds, especially in the southeast and among recent arrivals to urban Turkey, has driven substantial numbers toward religious movements as a political alternative. Kurds predominate among those apprehended in connection with the Istanbul bombings of November 2003. Certain areas of Turkey besides the southeast also have a reputation for religious conservatism. Konya, a traditional center of Sufi activism, is a leading example.

The Management of Islam

In the Turkish Republic, secularism does not mean just the separation of state and religion, as it does in most Western societies. The Kemalist state, drawing on Ottoman practice as well the French model of *laïcité*, insisted on the control of religion by state institutions. The republic inherited the mechanisms for the monitoring and regulation of religion that had been established by the Ottomans. The instrument for regulating Islam is the *Diyanet İşleri Başkanliği*, or Directorate of Religious Affairs, an office that reports to the prime minister and has a budget larger than that of most ministries. The *Diyanet* is the successor organization to the Ottoman office of Sheikh ul-Islam, but it differs in that the management of religious endowments was separated from the Ministry of Religious Affairs established by the first republican parliament and made the responsibility of a separate organization, a general directorate under the prime minister.

It is important to note that the *Diyanet* manages only the Sunni branch of Islam. It does not serve or organize other branches or other religions—which shows that the Turkish state, although secular, is not equidistant from all religions. Christianity and Judaism are not managed by a dedicated branch of government such as the *Diyanet*. They are self-governing but subject to Turkish laws and regulations, particularly those pertaining to minorities.

The *Diyanet* has two functions: the administration of Turkey's 77,000 mosques and the production of religious knowledge— "explaining Islam in the best way to people," as a *Diyanet* official put it. The *Diyanet* supervises the muftis, religious scholars who give legal opinions. Although religious officials are not supposed to involve themselves in politics, these opinions inevitably touch on controversial matters, such as the use of the headscarf. The *Diyanet's* position is that there is a religious requirement for women to cover themselves, especially at prayer, but that it is not a high priority in terms of religious duties.[10]

There is a mufti in each of Turkey's 81 provinces and 900 districts. All muftis and imams are state employees. They are educated in the *Imam-Hatip* schools, state religious-education institutions, and in any of the country's 20 faculties of theology. At the provincial level, muftis, preachers, and imams hold monthly meetings to discuss and prepare Friday sermons, although an imam can prepare his sermons alone if he wishes.

Within the *Diyanet*, a Religious Affairs High Board issues high-level decisions. Members of the board are selected by a group of delegates comprising professors of theology, muftis, and heads of *Diyanet* departments. The *Diyanet* also has a strong international presence, aimed at servicing the religious needs of Turks abroad. As of 2007, there were 528 imams in Germany and 90 in France, selected and prepared by the *Diyanet* in conjunction with German and French authorities. (The preparation includes instruction in the host country's lan-

---

[10] That has to be the *Diyanet's* position, since the Quran does instruct women to cover and mentions the headscarf in Nur 24:31.

guage and culture.) Overall, there are *Diyanet*-selected imams in 34 countries, including the United States, Canada, and Australia.[11]

Sufi Brotherhoods

Sufi orders, or brotherhoods (*tarikatlar*), such as the Bektaşi and the Safavi at one time competed with the Ottomans for the political control of eastern Anatolia, and Bektaşi Sufism eventually became the official order of the Janissaries. Although incorporated into the Sunni mainstream in Turkey, the sect maintained elements of heterodox Shi'a belief. Sufi orders have survived as important religious and social networks in modern Turkey, despite being outlawed and driven underground in the republican period. Two prominent *tarikatlar*, the Nakşibendi and the Kadiri, remain active on the Islamic scene, and their lodges often intersect with other business and political networks. The late Prime Minister and President Turgut Özal himself was a supporter of the İskenderpasa Nakşibendi Sufi order, and he promoted businessmen of Anatolian origin who had close ties to those circles.[12]

Since the 1950s, the *tarikatlar* have enjoyed a resurgence, including the formation of new orders, some of which have taken an active, if indirect, role in politics. (The Sufi resurgence was related to the change in the country's political leadership in 1950 from the Kemalist CHP to the conservative Democratic Party under Adnan Menderes, whose government was more tolerant of Islamic traditions.) Of Turkey's Sufi orders, the Nakşibendi has been the most visible, with political figures from Prime Ministers Özal to Erdoğan linked to the movement. There are more than a score of Nakşibendi groups in Turkey, each with its own sheikh, who is the undisputed leader of the group. Under the Ottomans, the Sufi orders had an umbrella organization, the *Majlis al-Mesheikh* (Council of Sheikhs), which was controlled by the state,

---

[11] Interview with Sabit Şimşek, Ankara, June 2007.

[12] M. Hakan Yavuz and John L. Esposito, *Turkish Islam and the Secular State: The Gülen Movement*, Syracuse, NY: Syracuse University Press, 2003, p. xxvi.

but this organization, together with the *tarikatlar,* was abolished by the republic.[13]

The Nakşibendi are known for their tolerance and flexibility. Members divide life into two spheres: the private and the religious. This leaves room for enjoying life. Some members have been known to indulge in moderate drinking in private; Özal, for example, drank at official dinners where alcohol was served. Erdoğan has reportedly been associated with the İsmail Ağa section of the Nakşibendi (named after the Istanbul mosque that bears the founder's name), a stricter branch. (Some people close to Erdoğan deny that he is affiliated with *tarikatlar* in any way; of course, Sufi orders are illegal in Turkey.) Abdullah Gül and former Speaker of Parliament Bülent Arınç also have Nakşibendi backgrounds.

The Nakşibendi were at the root of political Islam in Turkey. The first Turkish Islamist parties, Necmettin Erbakan's National Order Party (*Milli Nizam Partisi* (MNP)) and the National Salvation Party (*Milli Selamet Partisi* (MSP)) were established through the promotion and support of Sheikh Mehmet Zahid Kotku, the master of the Nakşibendi Khalidi *tarikat* centered at the İskenderpaşa mosque in Istanbul. Upon his death in 1980, Kotku was succeeded by his son-in-law, Professor Esad Coşan, who emphasized the strength of Islam as culture. In stressing "cultural" Islam, Özal diverged from Erbakan, who, in Coşan's view, had "excessively" politicized religion.[14]

In the 1980s, many Nakşibendi joined Turgut Özal's Motherland Party. Özal's brother, Korkut Özal, had created a political organization that brought together conservative and religious forces, the *Birlik Vakfi* (Unity Foundation). These connections carried over into the AKP. Recep Tayyip Erdoğan attended Sheikh Kotku's seminary at Iskanderpasa and gravitated toward the circle of Kotku and his successor Coşan. The political importance of the Sufi brotherhood,

---

[13] Interview with Süleyman Derin, Istanbul, June 2007.

[14] Şerif Mardin, "Turkish Islamic Exceptionalism Yesterday and Today," *Journal of International Affairs*, Vol. 54, No. 1, Fall 2000, pp. 158–159. See also "Biography of Prof. Dr. Mahmud Esad Coşan," at http://gumushkhanawidargah.8m.com/friday/mec.html (as of March 21, 2008).

according to Şerif Mardin, lies in these relationships. Brotherhoods are based on patronage, friendships, and associations, not on institutional influence. Usually they do not advertise what they do. Their mission is understood.[15]

Religious Movements

Economic and political liberalization during the administration of Turgut Özal facilitated the development of a "religious market" in Turkey. Nakşibendi orders, the Fethullah Gülen movement, and the political National View movement of Necmettin Erbakan competed over the meaning and proper role of Islam in Turkish society.[16] The Gülen movement has its roots in the Nurculuk movement of Said Nursi (1873–1960), who is best known as the author of the *Risale-i Nur*, the "Message of Light," a 6,000-page commentary on the Quran. He argued that the time of the "jihad of the sword" was over, and that we are now in the era of the "jihad of the word," meaning a reasoned attempt to reconcile science and rationalism with Islam. Nursi defended the rights of Armenians and Greeks in Turkey and reached out to Christian leaders. In 1950, he sent his collected works to Pope Pius XII and received in reply a personal letter of thanks. In the same way, in 1953, Nursi visited the Ecumenical Patriarch Athenagoras in Istanbul to seek cooperation between Muslims and Christians against atheism.[17]

Fethullah Gülen reinvented the Nur movement as "Turkish Islam." He departed from Nursi's emphasis on individual transformation and focused on the public sphere and on turning Islam into

---

[15] Ibid.; interview with Şerif Mardin, Istanbul, June 2007.

[16] Yavuz and Esposito, op. cit., pp. xxvi–xxvii.

[17] John L. Allen, Jr., "These two Islamic movements bear watching," *All Things Catholic*, National Catholic Reporter, June 22, 2007, at http://ncrcafe.org/node/1188 (as of March 21, 2008). See also Thomas Michel, S.J., "Muslim-Christian Dialogue and Cooperation in the Thought of Bediuzzaman Said Nursi," *The Muslim World*, Vol. 88, No. 3-4, July–October 1999, at http://www.blackwell-synergy.com/doi/pdf/10.1111/j.1478-1913.1999.tb02751.x (as of March 21, 2008).

Islamic networks and social capital.[18] The Gülen movement is active in promoting harmony among Islam, Christianity, and Judaism, and it sponsors a variety of fora for interfaith dialogue.[19] A web of organizations propagates Gülen's vision of Islam. These include Fatih University in Istanbul and an extensive network of schools, hospitals, and charitable and media organizations, including the mass-circulation newspaper *Zaman*, television stations *Samanyolu* (Milky Way) and *Mehtap* (Full Moon), and the English-language *Ebru* satellite television station in the United States. The movement's holdings include a news agency (*Cihan Haber Ajansı*); the English-language daily *Today's Zaman*; a weekly newsmagazine, *Aksiyon*; an Islamic finance institution, Bank Asya (formerly known as *Asya Finans*); and an insurance company, *Işık Sigorta*. "Asya" is Turkish for Asia and resonates with the Gülen movement's extensive presence in Asian countries.

The Journalists and Writers Foundation *(Gazeteciler ve Yazarlar Vakfı* (GYV), associated with the Gülen movement, sponsors several dialogue platforms, including the Abant Platform (named after the location in western Turkey where the conferences take place), which brings together intellectuals and scholars to discuss national and international problems;[20] the Eurasian Dialogue Platform, which includes representatives from Turkey and 12 countries in the former Soviet Union and Asia; and the Intercultural Dialogue Platform, which has organized Abrahamic meetings in Turkey, the Russian Federation, Georgia, Germany, and Sweden.

The GYV also runs a large publishing enterprise that publishes books by Gülen and other Turkish authors on historical and sociological subjects, as well as a quarterly magazine, *Da,* printed in Russian

---

[18] Yavuz and Esposito, op. cit., p. 19.

[19] The movement sponsored the performance of the traditional Mevlevi Sufi ritual by the Whirling Dervishes at the Washington Hebrew Congregation in June 2006, a remarkable presentation of an Islamic ritual in a Jewish religious setting.

[20] The Abant Platform has held international conferences in Washington, D.C., in collaboration with The Johns Hopkins University School of Advanced International Studies (SAIS); in Brussels, with the Catholic University of Louvain; in Paris, with UNESCO and the Sorbonne; and in Cairo, with the Al-Ahram Strategic Center.

and Turkish in Istanbul, Moscow, and Almaty.[21] According to GYV officials, the movement's emphasis on Eurasia is explained by Turkey's historical and cultural links to Turkic-speaking peoples in the Russian Federation and the Central Asian republics, where the Gülen movement has also established a large number of schools. It also reflects the interests of businessmen associated with the movement.[22]

The Gülen movement has also developed a very effective international network beyond Eurasia, with many adherents in the United States (where the movement's founder lives). The Washington-based Rumi Forum organizes several intercultural trips to Turkey each year for U.S. residents to familiarize them with Turkish culture and the social work of the Gülen movement in Turkey.[23] Secular Turks in mainstream Turkish-American organizations and in the Turkish Foreign Service often note that the secular Turkish diaspora is disorganized, fragmented, and inactive by comparison.

In addition to income from publishing, media, and financial enterprises associated with the Gülen movement, funding for the movement comes from donations by supporters, including wealthy Turkish businessmen. For example, one Gülen donor owns Ülker, Turkey's largest enterprise in many food sectors. The newspaper *Zaman* is owned by Ali Akbulut, a prominent textile manufacturer. According to GYV officials, their publishing enterprise also generates funding that is used to support the dialogue fora sponsored by the movement.[24]

The movement is viewed with considerable suspicion by secularists, who believe that it has an Islamist agenda. (In some ways, secularist views toward it parallel those toward the AKP.) According to some Turkish analysts, an important part of the AKP base is composed of Gülen supporters.[25] In the 1980s, Gülen adherents supported Turgut Özal, but the movement never supported Erbakan. After the February

---

[21] Interview with Cemal Uşak, Vice President, GYV, Istanbul, June 2005.

[22] More than 200 businessmen in Kazakhstan alone, according to Uşak.

[23] See the Rumi Forum web site, www.rumiforum.org.

[24] Interview with Cemal Uşak, Istanbul, June 2005.

[25] Interview with a well-informed Turkish journalist, Ankara, June 2007.

28, 1997, "soft coup" that removed Erbakan from office, the movement, through its media—*Zaman* and STV—supported the reformist movement that led to the establishment of the AKP.[26] Gülen himself moved to the United States in 1999 after he was indicted for allegedly plotting to subvert Turkey's secular state. He was acquitted in 2006 but has remained in the United States because his return to Turkey could become a political issue.[27]

Gülen's critics point to videotapes of his speeches that have surfaced as evidence of an intention to overthrow Turkey's secular order. In these videotapes, Gülen appears to counsel working slowly and diligently until the time comes to change the system.[28] His supporters say that his intention was to advise his followers not to open themselves to discrimination by an open display of religious conviction. Scholars such as İhsan Dağı believe that the movement does not have an Islamist agenda. Gülen's supporters are attracted, he says, to the Ottoman model of pluralism and tolerance and want to spread their influence. In this regard, he says, the movement has a convergence of interests with the AKP that involves replacing the Kemalist model of uncompromising secularism with a new synthesis that would make more room for religion, but not seeking to establish an Islamic state (a goal that the movement explicitly rejects).[29]

Islamic Foundations

Since Ottoman times, Turkey has had a tradition of Islamic foundations (*vakıflar*), and these remain a part of the Turkish scene in both

---

[26] Ibid.

[27] A Turkish source sympathetic to the Gülen movement told the authors that if Gülen were to return, secularists would liken it to the return of the Ayatollah Khomeini from France in 1979. To prevent problems for the government, the source told us, Gülen has decided to postpone his return. His health may also be a factor in his decision not to return at this time (authors' discussion in Istanbul, June 2007).

[28] The speeches (in Turkish) appear to have been made in the mid-1990s. The tapes are available on the Internet at http://www.youtube.com/watch?v=oNi3Z3qZ7Z4; http://www.youtube.com/watch?v=4tbnGnzdmgU; http://www.youtube.com/watch?v=SRAyGkE1q50 (as of March 21, 2008).

[29] Ihsan Dağı, "Turkish Politics at the Crossroads," presentation, February 8, 2007.

urban and provincial settings. They have been important in a society where the social-welfare capacity of the state has been limited and often ineffective in bringing social services to new urban migrants. The Islamist political parties, from Refah to Saadet, and above all, the AKP, have been especially active in this area. In a very real sense, these charitable and social-welfare activities have been the basis for the party's success at the municipal and national levels. As the AKP has become more entrenched in politics and society, it has also become more capable of raising charitable funds from like-minded (and some not so like-minded) contributors.

Islamic Schools

The proliferation of religious schools (*İmam-Hatip*) got under way in earnest during the Özal period. The *İmam-Hatip* schools were established in the 1950s as vocational schools to produce qualified religious personnel. Their curriculum combines training in secular subjects with courses in religion. The schools generated a great deal of controversy, which appeared to be settled by the end of the Refah government and the introduction of regulations limiting their role. In fact, however, the issue of the *İmam-Hatip* schools remains highly controversial. The AKP government has been placing *İmam-Hatip* graduates in government departments and state-owned firms at all levels of responsibility. This practice, along with the government's spring 2004 decision to introduce legislation aimed at giving the schools' graduates wider access to university and professional opportunities, spurred sharp opposition in secular circles. As Turks on both sides of the controversy are aware, the progressive introduction of AKP cadres, including *İmam-Hatip* graduates, into the state apparatus may be one of the leading vehicles for change in the secular-religious balance over time.

Shi'ites and Alevis

Turkey's religious tradition, while overwhelmingly orthodox and Sunni, has always had a strong non-Sunni Muslim minority with diverse underground sects. The population of eastern Anatolia was predominantly Shi'ite until the 16th century, when the Ottoman Empire, engaged in a struggle for regional preeminence with Safavid Persia, sought to distinguish itself from its Shi'ite rival by championing Sunni orthodoxy.

The Alevis, Turkey's leading religious minority, are a significant factor in Turkey's social and political climate.[30] There is considerable uncertainty about the numbers of Alevis in Turkey. According to some estimates, 70 percent of the non-Sunni Muslim minority of roughly 15 million are Alevis. (The other 30 percent are Shi'ites.) Other estimates are lower, in the range of 5 to 10 million. Most Alevis in Turkey are ethnic Turks, but the sect also includes most of Turkey's Arabs and perhaps a quarter of its Kurds. Alevis are sometimes confused with Shi'ites because they share some Shi'ite beliefs and practices, such as veneration of the Imam Ali and observance of the holy month of *Muharrem*, but in fact, they constitute a distinct religion and culture (see discussion below).

Alevism is a highly syncretic belief system with pre-Islamic Shamanistic and Zoroastrian elements, as well as strong Sufi influences (primarily from the Bektaşi school). Alevis differ from orthodox Muslims in that they observe different fasting days, do not attend mosques, do not follow the practice of daily prayers (or pray three times a day), and do not consider the *hajj* a religious obligation. The Alevis have meeting houses called *cem evleri*, which are a medium primarily of socialization and not of religious practice. They have unique institutions: the *dedelik, zakirlik,* and *on iki hizmet.*[31] Although as far as the Turkish state is concerned, the Alevis are Muslims, some Alevi intellectuals maintain that they are not Muslims at all, and that Alevism

---

[30] Not to be confused with Syria's Alawites, who are predominantly Arab and have different beliefs, founding saints, practices, and social structure.

[31] The *dede* is traditionally a religious leader whose authority derives from his charisma as a religious mystic and also from his status as an elder in the community; the *zakir* is also a religious authority; the *on iki hizmet* (twelve services) conducts services during mass prayers. Until recently, all of these positions were hereditary. Özlem Göner, "The Transformation of the Alevi Collective Identity," *Cultural Dynamics*, Vol. 17, No. 2, 2005, p. 132, fn 14, at http://cdy.sagepub.com/cgi/content/abstract/17/2/107 (as of March 21, 2008).

may in fact be not a religion, but a group identity.[32] The confusion about Alevism derives from the fact that it has not been systematized as a formalistic religion.[33] The Alevis have no systematic theology, no sacred books, and no *shari'a* tradition. For them, the important thing is the *tasavvuf*,[34] or internal experience. In this regard, their approach to religion is very much like that of the Sufis.

The Alevis supported the establishment of the secular republic, which severed the ties to Sunni Islam as a state religion and ended formal discrimination against Alevis, although the Kemalist policy of closing down the places of worship of religious sects adversely affected their religious practices. This is why some Alevis perceive Atatürk as the most important political figure in Alevi history. On the other hand, Göner argues that despite its secular nature, the republic maintained the privileged position of Sunni Islam as a defining characteristic of the Turkish identity and perpetuated the Alevis' status as outsiders.[35] After the 1960 coup, the Alevis became politically identified with left-wing parties. Marxism gained ground among younger Alevis, who began to redefine Alevism as a socialist movement and became the target of right-wing extremists. In the 1978 Kahramanmaraş incident, right-wing "Grey Wolves" killed about 100 left-wing Alevi activists.[36]

After the 1980 coup, what the prominent Turkish scholar of Alevism Reha Çamuroğlu calls "the Alevi renaissance" began. Alevis gradually abandoned socialist ideology and returned to the religious and

---

[32] The European Union categorizes Alevis as a "non-Sunni Muslim minority."

[33] However, Alevi foundations have made efforts to do just that. Özlem Göner saw the following announcement on the message board of the Karacaahmet Foundation: "Bring us all of those legends, stories and books that are the heritage of your grandfathers and your village, so that we will document them to codify our culture and religion." Göner, op. cit., p. 129.

[34] *Irfan* in Arabic or Persian.

[35] Göner, op. cit., pp. 111–113.

[36] Interview with Reha Çamuroğlu, Istanbul, June 2007. In 1993, Sunni extremists set fire to a hotel in Sivas where Alevi and pro-Alevi intellectuals had gathered. The police were criticized for inaction during this incident, in which 35 people were killed. See Stephen Kinzer, *Crescent and Star: Turkey Between Two Worlds*, New York: Farrar, Straus and Giroux, 2001, p. 64.

communitarian core of Alevism.[37] By and large, Alevi intellectuals and community leaders are secular in their behavior. The majority of them support the CHP, although they have an uncomfortable relationship with Turkey's secular establishment and the nationalist right, many of whose members tend to associate Alevis with leftist politics.[38] In the July 2007 parliamentary election, the Alevi Cem Foundation leader, Professor İzzettin Doğan, called on Alevis to vote for the CHP or other secular parties because, he said, the AKP intended to overthrow the country's secular order.[39]

There are a number of Alevi foundations that seek to promote Alevi cultural awareness and end official discrimination against Alevism—for example, by having the Alevi meeting houses designated as official houses of prayer.[40] The most important of these foundations is the Cem Foundation, mentioned above. The Ehl-i Beyt Foundation represents a strand of Alevism that is closer to Shi'a Islam—its adherents pray five times a day and go on the *hajj*.[41]

Turkish Attitudes Toward Religion

It has been assumed that most Turks identify themselves as Turks or citizens of the Turkish Republic first, and as Muslims second. However, a recent survey funded by the Turkish Economic and Social Stud-

---

[37] Interview with Reha Çamuroğlu, Istanbul, June 2007.

[38] In the 2007 parliamentary election, in a remarkable break with past patterns, Çamuroğlu was elected to parliament on the AKP ticket. He told us before the election that it was difficult for Erdoğan to invite him to join the ticket (because of prejudice against Alevis within the AKP base) and difficult for him to accept (because of Alevi prejudices against the AKP and Sunnis), but that he accepted because the AKP is trying to change from a moderate Islamist to a liberal party. Interview with Reha Çamuroğlu, Istanbul, June 2007.

[39] "Alevis vote based on individual decisions," *Today's Zaman*, July 18, 2007.

[40] "Alevis await decision on house of worship status for cem evleri," *Today's Zaman*, June 22, 2007, at http://www.todayszaman.com/tz-web/detaylar.do?load=detay&link=114687 (as of March 21, 2008). The official view is that since Alevis (in the state's view) are Muslims, they should pray in mosques.

[41] Interview with Hüseyin Özcan, Fatih University, Istanbul, June 2007.

ies Foundation (TESEV), in which 1,500 interviews were conducted in 23 provinces, pointed to a striking increase in the sense of Muslim identity as a component of Turkishness (see Table 2.1).

Interpreting the poll, TESEV Board of Directors Chairman Can Paker posited that Turks divide into two sociopolitical parts: one-third of them are secular, and two-thirds are religious. Of secular Turks, about 10 percent are ultrasecularists, very nationalistic, anti-Europe, and increasingly anti–United States. The other 20 percent are democratic and deeply concerned that Turkish secularism could be lost—that there could be a gradual erosion of secular rights and that over time Turkey could be "Iranized." Of the religious Turks, some 10 percent are in favor of a state based on *shari'a* (Islamic law); 50 to 60 percent are conservative, but they also want to be modern, and they have middle-class aspirations. The religious divide does not align clearly with geographic lines. People in eastern Anatolia, for example, are more socially conservative, but not necessarily more religious than those in western Turkey. Support for *shari'a* law is not greater in eastern Anatolia than in the suburbs of some of Turkey's largest cities.[42]

Table 2.1
Turks' Primary Identity

Primary Identity	Percentage of Respondents
Turk	19.4
Muslim	44.6
Citizen of Turkish Republic	29.9
Kurd	2.7
Alevi	1.1
Other	1.3
No reply	1.0

SOURCE: Ali Çarkoğlu and Binnaz Toprak, *Değişen Türkiye 'de Din, Toplum ve Siyaset*, Istanbul: TESEV, 2006.

---

[42] Interview with Can Paker, Istanbul, June 2007.

The survey confirms the widespread impression that Turks are becoming more religious, but it also shows that the vast majority of Turks oppose a state based on religion: 76 percent of the respondents opposed the implementation of *shari'a*, while only 9 percent favored it. In 1995, 27 percent favored it. Among AKP voters, 70 percent opposed *shari'a* and 14 percent favored it. This was a higher proportion than among the population at large, but still a small minority.[43] A large majority (81.9 percent, but only 60 percent of AKP voters) said they believed that people are able to exercise Islamic practices freely. That is to say, four-fifths of the respondents were satisfied that the secular state did not interfere with the practice of religion. Those who took the opposite view (40 percent of the AKP voters) gave the headscarf issue as the predominant example of the oppression of religious people by the state.[44]

An interesting finding of the TESEV survey concerns the qualifications that people would like their president to have. In the respondents' view, these qualifications should include:[45]

- Having an exemplary lifestyle for modern Turkey (86 percent of respondents)
- Being a devout Muslim (74 percent)
- Being a guardian of secularity (75 percent).

---

[43] Ibid. The 2006 TESEV study (Çarkoğlu and Toprak, 2006) also references other studies that asked a similar question and found that *shari'a* was supported by 29 percent in 1995, 27 percent in 1996, 20 percent in 1998, and 16 percent in 2002. While these other surveys are not exactly comparable to TESEV's, they seem to confirm that support for *shari'a* has been waning steadily since the mid-1990s. However, the TESEV report also presents intriguing results on another survey item. Asked whether there should be religion-based political parties, 25 percent said "Yes" in 1999, and 41 percent said "Yes" in 2006. "No" responses declined from 61 percent in 1999 to 54 percent in 2006. "Don't know/no response" fell from 15 percent in 1999 to 5 percent in 2006. This suggests that the AKP has won additional sympathizers to its stance.

[44] Interview with Can Paker, Istanbul, June 2007.

[45] Other qualifications cited were the ability to capture public opinion (89 percent); knowledge of and experience in foreign affairs (87 percent); education in the law (83 percent); and wife's head being not covered (50 percent). The broader message in the survey is that Turks care more about statesmanlike qualities than about controversial Islam/secularity issues when it comes to selecting their president. Çarkoğlu and Toprak, op. cit., 2006.

Clearly, Turks do not see a contradiction between being a good Muslim and being secular. This is consistent with Turks' conception of who is a Muslim, which involves high tolerance. Of the survey respondents, 66 percent agreed that those who drank alcohol were Muslims (although 71 percent agreed that alcohol should be banned during Ramadan); 85 percent considered an uncovered woman a Muslim; 29 percent said they would be disturbed if miniskirted women were in the majority in the neighborhood, while 66 percent were undecided; 13 percent said they would be disturbed if covered women were in the majority in the neighborhood, with a large majority (84 percent) undecided; 89 percent thought that there can be "good" people among believers of other religions, but only 42 percent believed that non-Muslims could go to heaven (provided they have not sinned).[46] On the other hand, minority rights of Kurds, Alevis, and non-Muslims found very little support. The TESEV survey also confirms that the vast majority of Turks oppose terrorism. A large majority (65.5 percent) oppose suicide attacks even against "occupation" (20.2 percent support them); and 82 percent oppose Palestinian suicide attacks against civilians (8.3 percent support them). Further, 56 percent agree that the 9/11 attacks cannot be justified from an Islamic point of view (22 percent disagree).[47]

The TESEV survey has touched off a lively debate in Turkey and among Turkey-watchers about what the results actually indicate. That Turks are more open in discussing their Muslim identity takes few observers by surprise, but the survey leaves much open to interpretation, including the distinction between religiosity and attitudes toward religion in politics. The debate is often couched in terms of the "secular-Islamist divide." But many Turks argue that the real divide in Turkish politics today is not between secularists and Islamists, but rather between nationalists (or statists) and reformers. Ali Çarkoğlu, one of the co-authors of the 2006 TESEV study, believes that the bottom line of the report is that there is potential in Turkey to pursue religious issues from a liberal perspective.[48]

---

[46] The tolerance data are from the 2000 TESEV study (Ali Çarkoğlu and Binnaz Toprak, *Türkiye'de Din, Toplum ve Siyaset,* Istanbul: TESEV, 2000).

[47] Çarkoğlu and Toprak, 2006.

[48] Ali Çarkoğlu, presentation, op. cit.

The Violent Fringe

For historical and cultural reasons, Turkey has been more resistant to radical and violent varieties of Islamism than other Muslim societies have. Nevertheless, Turkey has not been immune to the infiltration of radical Salafi ideologies. Interestingly, radical Islamism entered the Turkish politico-religious stream by way of Europe. In the 1980s, Cemalettin Kaplan, the former mufti of Adana and deputy head of the *Diyanet*, the Directorate of Religious Affairs, for several years, was granted political asylum in Germany, where he founded the *Islami Cemaatler ve Cemiyetler Birliği* (Union of Islamic Communities and Societies), with the aim of establishing a theocratic state in Turkey. In 1993, Kaplan's organization became the *Anadolu Federe Islam Devleti* (Federated Islamic State of Anatolia). Upon Cemalettin Kaplan's death in 1995, his son Metin became the self-styled "caliph" of the extremist organization, which he ran until he was extradited to Turkey in 2004.[49]

Currently, the major sources of radical Islamist violence in Turkey are Turkish Hezballah and al-Qaeda. Although Turkish Hezballah has declined since the death of its leader Hüseyin Velioğlu in a shootout with police in January 2000, al-Qaeda–linked cells retain the potential to carry out terrorist attacks. Neither group, however, is connected to any significant sector of Turkish Muslim society.

Turkish Hezballah (not to be confused with Lebanese Hezballah) was established in southeastern Anatolia in the 1980s. Although largely a Kurdish Sunni group, it was influenced by the Iranian revolution and for a time received logistical and financial support from Iran. Turkish Hezballah's goal was the establishment of an Islamic state through a strategy of stages, the last of which was armed struggle (jihad) to remove the forces of unbelief. Its main target, however, was not the state, but the PKK, which gained the organization some degree of tolerance from the authorities. In the 1990s, it began to expand into western Turkey, where it carried out a number of assassinations. The organization went

---

[49] "Is a New Wave of Terrorism Starting Against Turkey?" *Pulse of Turkey*, No. 68, November 7, 1998, at http://www.turkpulse.com/is.htm (as of March 21, 2008).

into decline after the security forces killed Velioğlu and captured other senior leaders. Turkish Hezballah has not conducted a major operation since the assassination of the Diyarbakır police chief, Gaffar Okkan, and five other officers in 2001.[50]

A Turkish al-Qaeda cell carried out two sets of attacks in Istanbul in November 2003: the bombings of the Beth Israel and Neve Shalom synagogues and, five days later, of the British consulate general and the HSBC Bank headquarters. According to Turkish prosecutors, the bombings were orchestrated by a senior al-Qaeda operative, Syrian Louai Sakka (aka Louai al-Turki), with specific approval from Osama bin Laden and Abu Musab al-Zarqawi. Sakka was arrested in August 2005 after a bomb he had been assembling blew up in an apartment in Antalya.[51]

Since then, there have been further arrests of al-Qaeda suspects. Eleven were arrested in Istanbul in May 2007, and 23 were arrested in Bursa in June 2007. In September 2007, the Turkish police foiled a massive bombing attack in Ankara. A van in a multistory parking lot in the Kurtulus neighborhood of the city was found to contain a 580-kilogram improvised explosive device (IED) consisting of ammonium nitrate, sodium nitrate, TNT, and 20 small LPG bottles, to which three cell phones were connected, suggesting that the perpetrators planned to detonate the device remotely. Although the authorities have directed their investigation at the PKK, the device most closely resembles those used in the November 2003 Istanbul bombings.[52]

Turks in Europe

The large-scale migration of Turks to Western Europe, especially Germany, and the establishment of large Turkish communities in Europe

---

[50] See M. Kürşad Atalar, "Hizballah of Turkey: A Pseudo-Threat to the Secular Order?" *Turkish Studies*, Vol. 7, No. 2, July 2006, p. 311.

[51] "A bomb-builder, 'out of the shadows,'" *The Washington Post*, February 20, 2006.

[52] The PKK has no record of using large, vehicle-borne IEDs, nor does it have a tradition of mass-casualty terrorist attacks. See "Turkish Police No Nearer to Solving Attempted Ankara Bombing," *Eurasia Daily Monitor*, Vol. 4, Issue 172, September 18, 2007.

with intimate ties to the homeland but outside of the purview of Turkish authorities have affected Turkey as a whole in profound ways.

According to German census data, in 2000, there were 1,998,534 non-citizen Turks in Germany,[53] comprising 2.5 percent of the total population. The Turkish population in Germany is relatively conservative, traditional, and religious. Kurds also make up a relatively large part—perhaps one-third—of this community. It is a significant feature of Turkish political Islam that many of the more extreme movements are in Europe rather than in Turkey itself.

The explanation for this resides in part with the more religious and conservative nature of Turkish migrants to Europe. It also reflects the relative ease with which extremist groups—both Islamic and Kurdish—have been able to organize and operate outside the reach of Turkish courts and security agencies. Only in the post-9/11 climate of increased scrutiny and more frequent prosecutions has this situation begun to change, with radical groups outside Turkey coming under increasing pressure from terrorism-conscious European governments.

The main Turkish radical groups active in Germany are *Milli Görüş* (National View) and *Kalifatsstaat*, also known as the Kaplan Group. *Milli Görüş* is the European offshoot of Necmettin Erbakan's series of political parties, as well as a concept in Turkish Islamist domestic politics. It has always been a key theme of Erbakan's rhetoric, and it dates back to the pre-Refah period, when he led his original National Order Party (*Milli Nizam Partisi* (MNP)). Although never defined clearly, the party's motto was used to emphasize the difference between Erbakan's line and that of other parties that were, in his words, "imitators of the West." Today's Felicity Party *(Saadet Partisi* (SP))*, which continues the MNP legacy and is run by Erbakan protégé Recai Kutan, still uses *Milli Görüş* rhetoric. The phrase is also embraced by political Islamists in Europe as a way to imply adherence to the Erbakan way. In Germany, *Milli Görüş* has a membership of 26,500, but according to German authorities, the group reaches a far larger audience throughout Europe through the 514 mosque communities it operates (including 323 in Germany); its newspaper, *Milli*

---

[53] *Statistisches Bundesamt Deutschland*, December 31, 2000.

Gazete (actually the European edition of the Turkish paper of the same name); and its extensive Islamic education programs.[54]

The more radical *Kalifatsstaat* (Kaplan Group), led by the self-declared *Emirs der Glaeubigen und Kalifen der Muslime*, Metin Kaplan, has as its goal destroying the secular state in Turkey and replacing it with an Islamic state based on *shari'a* law. Kaplan's followers were involved in a plot to crash an airplane into the Atatürk Mausoleum in Ankara on the 75th anniversary of the Turkish Republic. The *Kalifatsstaat* and its associated organizations were declared illegal by German authorities in 2004, and Kaplan was arrested and convicted of soliciting the assassination of a rival preacher, Ibrahim Sofu, in 1996. After serving a four-year sentence, Kaplan was extradited to Turkey in 2004, where he was sentenced to life imprisonment.[55] German authorities estimate that the Kaplan Group has a membership of 750 in Germany.[56]

Until recently, Turks in Europe have by and large not been involved in terrorism.[57] However, in September 2007, German authorities broke up a terrorist ring that was plotting attacks against U.S. military installations in Germany and Frankfurt Airport. One of the individuals arrested was a 28-year-old Turk, Adem Yilmaz, who had trained in an al-Qaeda camp in Pakistan in March 2006. The Turkish dimension of the plot has shaken Germans, who have long taken comfort in the belief that their Muslim community—which is mostly composed of Turks—was less prone to terrorism or radical Islamic ideas than Islamic communities elsewhere in Europe were. Yilmaz came from a largely middle-class background and had spent most of his life in Germany. Like many of the younger Turks born in Germany, he rejected the established mosque sponsored by the Turkish government in favor of a more radical independent mosque.[58]

---

[54] See data on *Milli Görüş* in *Verfassungsschutzbericht 2005*, published by Bundesministerium des Innern, Berlin, May 2006, at www.verfassungsschutz.de (as of March 21, 2008).

[55] *Verfassungsschutzbericht 2005*.

[56] Bundesverfassungsschutzamt, *Jahresbericht*, 2004.

[57] This statement refers to ethnic Turks, not to Turkish Kurds associated with the PKK.

[58] Mark Landler and Nicholas Kulish, "Turkish connection shakes Germans," *International Herald Tribune*, September 8–9, 2007.

Quite apart from the issue of Islamic radicalism among Turks abroad, there is the larger question of why many second- and even third-generation Turks in Germany and elsewhere have been attracted to Islamist movements. For some analysts, the answer is not simply the more traditional social outlook brought from provincial Turkey. Younger émigré Turks may be turning to Islam as a reaction to perceived discrimination by and alienation from the host society.[59] Many supporters of *Milli Görüs,* as well as adherents of the Kaplan Group, have been drawn from this sector.[60] Given the size of the Turkish community in Germany, it is not surprising that most of the leading tendencies in contemporary Turkish political Islam are represented by sister organizations in Germany. This has also been true of various Kurdish movements, both violent and nonviolent, whose financing has relied heavily on émigré sources.

Kurdish groups are also active in Europe. The PKK reportedly gets the bulk of its financing from the drug trade. British security officials estimate that the PKK smuggles 40 percent of the heroin going from the East into the EU annually, calculated to be worth $5 billion by the United Nations Office for Drugs and Crime. The PKK's fundraising activities also include the trafficking of illegal immigrants.[61]

---

[59] See Werner Schiffauer, "Islamism in the Diaspora: The Fascination of Political Islam Among Second Generation German Turks," unpublished paper, Frankfurt/Oder: Europea-Universität Viadrina, 1999. Until recently, Germany did not bestow citizenship on non-ethnic German residents upon birth. In 1999, the German government passed a law that became effective in 2000, bestowing citizenship on persons born in Germany whose parents had been residents for the previous eight years or had had permanent legal-resident status for at least three years. However, these people must make a choice between German and Turkish citizenship when they reach the age of 23. Deutsche Botschaft Ankara, at http://www.ankara.diplo.de/Vertretung/ankara/tr/01/stag.html (as of March 21, 2008).

[60] See Schiffauer, op. cit., pp. 5–6.

[61] Soner Cagaptay, "Can the PKK Renounce Violence? Terrorism Resurgent," *Middle East Quarterly*, Winter 2007, pp. 45–52, available at http://www.meforum.org/article/1060 (as of March 21, 2008).

CHAPTER THREE

The Rise of Political Islam in Turkey

Over the past several decades, the strength of Islamism, or political Islam, has been growing in Turkey. Prior to 1970, the religious right was just a faction within the mainstream center-right parties. In the 1970s, it emerged as a separate political movement under the leadership of Necmattin Erbakan, who founded the *Milli Görüş* movement. Islamic parties have faced strong scrutiny by the Kemalist authorities and were banned or closed down on several occasions. However, they have recently reemerged in various guises, attesting to their durability and ability to attract an important segment of the Turkish electorate. Still, until recently, they remained largely a fringe movement.

The success of the AKP, which has Islamic roots, in the two most recent national elections, however, demonstrates the growing strength of political Islam. In the November 2002 elections, the AKP won 34 percent of the vote, enabling it to govern on its own. In the July 2007 election, it fared even better, winning 46.6 percent of the vote, more than twice that of the CHP, the party representing the Atatürk secular tradition, which came in second with 20.9 percent of the vote.[1]

This is a remarkable achievement for a party that did not exist before August 2001, and it underscores the degree to which a form of political Islam has moved out of the political shadows to become a major actor in Turkish politics. The AKP defines itself as a "conservative democratic" party, not as an Islamist party, but many Kemalists fear that it has a hidden Islamic agenda and that its ascendancy poses

---

[1] In alliance with the smaller, left-of-center Democratic Left Party (*Demokratik Sol Parti* (DSP)). In 2002, the CHP won 19.4 percent of the vote, and the DSP won 1.2 percent.

a threat to the secularist nature of the Turkish state. What explains the rise of religion-based politics in Turkey? Does the AKP's success represent a "re-Islamization" of Turkish political life and foreign policy? What are its implications for Turkey's political development and foreign-policy orientation?

The Impact of the Kemalist Revolution

The rise of political Islam in Turkey has its roots in the reforms undertaken in the late Ottoman period and in the nature of the political transformation undertaken after the founding of the Turkish Republic by Mustafa Kemal Atatürk in 1923.[2] Atatürk's attempt to transform Turkey into a modern, Western, secular state essentially represented a "revolution from above." It was a state-instituted, top-down enterprise in social engineering carried out by a small military-bureaucratic elite that imposed its secularist vision on a reluctant traditional society. In carrying out this transformation, the elite made little effort to co-opt or cajole the population or the opposition. As Doğu Ergil noted, "Neither the secularization nor the Turkification of the nation was negotiated with the people in a serious way."[3] Instead the elite simply tried to use the "strong state" to overwhelm and intimidate any opposition.[4]

---

[2] There were important elements of continuity between the Westernization efforts undertaken in the late Ottoman period and those carried out by the Kemalists. Both were elitist, state-driven, and hostile to the development of autonomous groups and civil society. For a detailed discussion, see Metin Heper, "The Ottoman Legacy and Turkish Politics," *Journal of International Affairs*, Vol. 54, No. 1, Fall 2000, pp. 62–82. See also Şerif Mardin, "Center-Periphery Relations: A Key to Turkish Politics?" *Daedalus*, Vol. 102, Winter 1973, pp. 169–190. For a comprehensive discussion of the founding of the Turkish Republic and its early political transformation, see Bernard Lewis, *The Emergence of Modern Turkey*, London: Oxford University Press, 1968; Lord Kinross, *Atatürk*, New York: William Morrow, 1964; and Andrew Mango, *Atatürk*, New York: The Overlook Press, 1999.

[3] Doğu Ergil, "Identity Crises and Political Instability in Turkey," *Journal of International Affairs*, Vol. 54, No. 2, Fall 2000, p. 53.

[4] On the concept of the "strong state" and its use by the Kemalist elite in the modernization process, see in particular Henri J. Barkey, "The Struggles of a 'Strong' State," *Journal of International Affairs*, Vol. 54, No. 2, Fall 2000, pp. 87–105, and Metin Heper, "The Problem

The new Kemalist elite sought a radical break with the Ottoman past. The Ottoman era and everything associated with it, except a few elements of past grandeur, were condemned and discarded in favor of a new project based on Westernization and secularism. In the first decade after the founding of the republic, the Kemalists carried out a series of reforms that severed Turkey's ties to its Islamic past and to the Islamic world more broadly. The caliphate, led by the spiritual head of the Muslim Sunni world, was abolished. The Latin alphabet (modified to accommodate Turkish sounds) was introduced in place of Arabic script, and an effort was made to purge the Turkish language of words of Arabic and Persian origin that had migrated into it during the Ottoman period. The elite discouraged traditional attire and secularized the education system. All religious institutions and resources were brought under the control of the state.

However, most of these reforms were limited to the urban centers; the countryside remained largely untouched. Until the 1950s, the bulk of the Turkish population remained isolated and traditional, while the urban centers were modern and secular. In effect, two Turkeys coexisted in uneasy harmony: an urban, modern, secular "center" and a rural, traditional, religious "periphery,"[5] with little contact between them. The dominant elite was urban, modern, and secular, while the greater part of the population was rural, traditional, and pious.

Religion was not completely suppressed or eliminated. It was simply banished from the public sphere and strictly subordinated to and supervised by the state, through the Directorate of Religious Affairs (*Diyanet*). In effect, religious institutions became appendages of the state, with their personnel acting as civil servants. In the countryside, however, Islam continued to have strong social roots and remained largely beyond state control despite a ban on religious orders (*tarikatlar*) introduced in 1925.

---

of the Strong State for the Consolidation of Democracy," *Comparative Political Studies*, Vol. 25, July 1992, pp. 169–194.

[5] For a detailed discussion of the "center-periphery" dichotomy and its impact on Turkish politics, see Mardin, "Center-Periphery Relations: A Key to Turkish Politics?" pp. 169–190.

Indeed, a kind of religious "counterculture" existed outside the cities. In response to their forced exclusion from the political sphere, many Muslims established their own informal networks and educational systems. The religious networks and brotherhoods such as the Nakşibendi and the Nurculuk movement became a kind of "counter-public sphere" and the incubator of a more popular Islamic identity. Islam, as Hakan Yavuz has noted, remained the "hidden identity of the Kemalist state" and provided the vernacular for the marginalized majority excluded from the top-down transformation.[6]

Like its Ottoman predecessor, the Kemalist state discouraged the development of autonomous groups outside the control of the state. Autonomous activity, especially religious activity, was regarded by the state as a potential threat to its ability to carry out its modernization effort and consolidate its political control. Dissent or opposition to the regime's nationalist ideology and modernization policies was quickly suppressed. This attempt to suppress expressions of autonomous activity outside the control of the state not only alienated the large majority of the rural population, for whom religion was an important part of daily life, it also hindered the development of civil society more generally.[7]

The Kemalist state's modernization efforts provoked resistance among certain groups, particularly the Kurds. During the early years of the Turkish Republic, the new state faced a series of rebellions by the Kurds, who, accustomed to the Ottoman Empire's more tolerant attitude toward ethnicity and Islam, opposed the regime's emphasis on Turkish nationalism and secularism. These rebellions mixed ethnicity with religion and were a consequence of the unhinging of Anatolian society by Kemalist modernization policies.[8]

---

[6] Hakan Yavuz, "Cleansing Islam from the Public Sphere," *Journal of International Affairs*, Vol. 54, No. 1, Fall 2000, pp. 21–42.

[7] See Binnaz Toprak, "The State, Politics and Religion in Turkey," in Metin Heper and Ahmet Evin (eds.), *State, Democracy and the Military. Turkey in the 1980s*, Berlin/New York: Walter de Gruyter, 1988, pp. 119–136.

[8] Interestingly, the first of these rebellions, the Şeyh Said Rebellion in 1925, was redefined by the regime as a religious rebellion to bring back the caliphate—not a Kurdish rebellion. See Barkey, op. cit., p. 91.

After Atatürk's death in 1938, the authoritarian tendencies of the regime intensified. Atatürk's successor, İsmet İnönü, sought to build the regime's legitimacy on a strict interpretation of Kemalism. One-party rule served as a means to carry out a radical transformation of Turkish society. The majority of the population remained outside of politics and wedded to traditional habits and lifestyles over which Islam continued to exert an important influence.

In a sense, what has occurred over the past several decades is an attempt by this marginalized periphery to find its political voice and representation. Political Islam has increasingly provided that voice. Over time, the political goals and ideology of the Islamic movement have evolved, and it has jettisoned or moderated many key tenets of its initial political agenda, particularly its hostility to Westernization, in an effort to attract broader political support.

The Advent of Multiparty Democracy

The establishment of a multiparty system in 1946 was an important turning point in the rise of political Islam in Turkey. With the establishment of this system, the CHP (the party representing Kemalism) lost its monopoly on power. Thereafter, parties were forced to compete for power, and Islam became an important factor in attracting votes. The pious rural periphery, which had largely been excluded from politics since the founding of the republic in 1923, now became an important political constituency whose interests had to be taken into consideration by conservative political parties. At the same time, the CHP, which had ruled unopposed for more than two decades, was forced to adopt a more tolerant attitude toward Islam.

In 1950, the Democratic Party (DP), which was headed by Adnan Menderes, won a parliamentary majority, ending the CHP's monopoly of power. The DP was much less wedded to Kemalist conceptions of the state and appealed to those parts of society that felt marginalized and aggrieved by secularized Westernization policies. The DP promised to end some of the draconian secularist policies instituted by the Kemalist regime and also to reduce some of the cultural restrictions imposed on the Kurds. In effect, the DP "relegitimized Islam and traditional rural values."[9] As a result, these groups gradually were drawn into the competitive political arena for the first time. At the same time, Menderes' more liberal economic policies involved a limited movement away from the state-driven economic model.

Menderes' policies, though hardly revolutionary, were regarded as heretical and dangerous by many Kemalists and prompted the Turkish military to intervene in 1960 in the first of several coups. The military turned power back over to the politicians in 1961 and returned to the barracks—but only after instituting a number of reforms that strengthened its political role. One of the most important reforms was the creation of the National Security Council (MGK), a body dominated by the military and entrusted with ensuring that the government's domestic and foreign policies were in line with the basic tenets of the Kemalist revolution, particularly secularism. While technically an advisory body, the MKG institutionalized the role of the military in the political process and provided a mechanism by which the military could transmit its views directly to the civilian leadership.

At the same time, the 1961 constitution expanded the scope for associational freedom, which led to the proliferation of autonomous groups, including religious groups. Religious organizations that had resurfaced in the 1960s mushroomed in the 1970s. Different Sufi *tarikatlar* and religious networks helped the poor cope with the problems of modernization and became clubs for dislocated groups seeking solidarity in a rapidly changing world.[10] In this less-restrictive environment, religious forces were able to form their own separate political party, the National Order Party (MNP), the first in a series of religious parties established under the leadership of Necmettin Erbakan.

The Menderes era thus had several important results. First, it expanded the process of democratization and opened up the political arena to religious and ethnic groups that had previously been margin-

---

[9] Mardin, "Center-Periphery Relations: A Key to Turkish Politics?" p. 185.

[10] Ergil, "Identity Crises and Political Instability in Turkey," p. 54.

alized or excluded from politics. Second, it provided political space for religious groups to resurface and begin to organize politically.

The "Turkish-Islamic Synthesis"

Ironically, the military contributed to the strengthening of political Islam in Turkey. An upsurge of left-wing and right-wing violence that brought Turkey to the brink of civil war in the 1970s eventually prompted the military to intervene in 1980 to restore order.[11] In an effort to combat communism and leftist ideologies, the military attempted to strengthen the role of Islam. Under the military's tutelage, religious education was made a compulsory subject in all schools. Quranic classes were opened, and state-controlled moral and religious education was promoted.

In effect, the military sought to institute a process of state-controlled "Islamization from above." By fusing Islamic symbols with nationalism, the military hoped to create a more homogeneous and less political Islamic community and to insulate the population from the influence of left-wing ideologies. Based on the tripod of "the family, the mosque, and the barracks," this new "Turkish-Islamic synthesis" was designed to reduce the appeal of radical leftist ideologies and also to diminish the influence of non-Turkish strands of Islamic thinking from Pakistan and the Arab world.[12] The military also hoped the new synthesis would act as a counter to Islamic radicalism from Iran.

In composing this new synthesis, the military drew on the work of a group of conservative scholars who belonged to *Aydınlar Ocağı* (Intellectuals' Hearth). This association promulgated a moral and philosophical rationale for the synthesis, building an ideology out of Ottoman, Islamic, and Turkish popular culture to legitimize the hegemony

---

[11] For a detailed discussion of the coup and the events that prompted it, see Mehmet Ali Birand, *The Generals' Coup in Turkey*, London: Brassey's Defense Publishers, 1987.

[12] Cemal Karakas, *Turkey: Islam and Laïcism Between the Interests of the State, Politics and Society*, Report No. 78, Peace Research Institute Frankfurt (PRIF), 2007, pp. 17–18.

of the new ruling elite.[13] Reinterpreting the nation and state as a family and community, these scholars selectively used Ottoman-Islamic ideas to make the past relevant to the present and to cement differing interests together by emphasizing the danger to family, nation, and state posed by ideological fragmentation. The educational system and the media were then used to disseminate a popularized version of the ideology to the masses.

The architects of this ideological program hoped to create a new form of depoliticized Turkish-Islamic culture that would reunify society and provide the basis for a unified, strong, and stable state. The synthesis, however, sent an ambiguous message. On one hand, under the 1982 constitution, Turkey was defined as a secular state. On the other hand, the role of religion was strengthened in schools and education as a means of reinforcing Turkish nationalism, which tended to weaken the emphasis on secularism. At the same time, it provided opportunities for the Islamists to expand and reinforce their own message.

The Impact of the Özal Reforms

The economic and political reforms carried out under Prime Minister Turgut Özal in the mid-1980s also contributed to strengthening the role of Islamic groups. The reforms weakened the state's control over the economy and created a new class of entrepreneurs and capitalists in the provincial towns of Anatolia, including Denizli, Gaziantep, and Kahramanmaraş. The economic upswing created a new middle class—the so-called "Anatolian bourgeoisie"—with strong roots in Islamic culture. This group favors liberal economic policies and a reduction of the role of the state in the economic and social spheres. It also supports

---

[13] Hakan Yavuz, "Political Islam and the Welfare (Refah) Party in Turkey," *Comparative Politics*, Vol. 10, No. 1, October 1997, p. 68; for the Ottoman and republican origins of the "Turkish-Islamic synthesis," see Gökhan Çetinsaya, "Rethinking Nationalism and Islam: Some Preliminary Notes on the Roots of 'Turkish-Islamic Synthesis' in Modern Turkish Political Thought," *The Muslim World*, Vol. 89, Issue 3-4, October 1999, pp. 350–376, at http://www.blackwell-synergy.com/doi/abs/10.1111/j.1478-1913.1999.tb02753.x (as of March 21, 2008).

greater religious freedom. In the 1990s, it supported the Welfare Party. Today, it is one of the core constituencies backing the AKP.

Özal's reforms also resulted in an inflow of capital, much of it from the Arab world. This allowed the Islamists to organize politically. Under Özal's more tolerant approach to religion, Muslim groups and brotherhoods were given greater freedoms and were allowed to finance the construction of private schools and universities. The reforms also opened up greater political space for new political groups—including the Islamists. Islamist groups gained access to important media outlets and newspaper chains, which allowed them to reach a much broader political audience.[14] Television, in particular, provided an important means of propagating their message.[15]

Demographic changes also had an impact. The industrial and modernization policies pursued by successive Turkish governments led to a large-scale influx of the rural population into the cities. These rural migrants brought with them their traditional habits, beliefs, and customs. Uprooted and alienated, many lived in makeshift shanty-towns (*gecekondu mahallesi*) on the outskirts of large cities and were not integrated into urban culture. They represented an important pool of potential voters for Islamic parties opposed to Westernization and the forces of globalization, such as the series of Erbakan's *Milli Görüş* parties (see below). At the same time, the large influx of migrants contributed to an internal "clash of civilizations." The two Turkeys—one secular and urban, the other rural and pious—were brought into closer proximity with one another, exacerbating social tensions.

In many ways, Özal embodied these clashing traditions. A Western-trained technocrat who had worked for the World Bank, he was also a supporter of the Nakşibendi order and had been associated with Erbakan's National Salvation Party before founding the Motherland Party (*Anavatan Partisi* (ANAP)) in 1983. He thus bridged the

---

[14] Şerif Mardin has pointed to the important role played by the expansion of the media in propagating the "Islamic voice" and contributing to the rise of Islamic political parties. See Mardin, "Turkish Islamic Exceptionalism Yesterday and Today," p. 157.

[15] Until 1989, Turkey had only one television channel, the state-run TRT. The first religiously oriented channels began to emerge in 1993 and were linked to the Gülen movement.

secular-Islamic divide. As Henri Barkey noted, "He was as comfortable with Western leaders as in a mosque."[16]

The Rise of the Religious Right

These economic and social changes contributed to an upsurge in the political strength of Islamic political groups in the 1970s and 1980s. Its first independent political expression was the establishment of the National Order Party (MNP) in January 1970. The MNP was the first of several Islamic parties led by Necmettin Erbakan. It advocated a new economic and social order based on "national" (read Islamic) principles. However, the MNP's existence was short-lived. The party was shut down after a military intervention in 1971 on the grounds that it was against the secular nature of the state.

The founders of the MNP and its successors came out of the National View (*Milli Görüş*) movement,[17] whose leaders sought a return to traditional values and institutions. They regarded the Kemalist attempt to replace the Islamic-Ottoman state and culture with a Western model as a historic mistake and the source of all the ills in Turkish society. Their goal was to build a "national (Islamic) order" and put an end to the process of Westernization.[18] They saw Turkey's identity and future closely linked with the Muslim world, rather than with the West.

The National Salvation Party (*Milli Selamet Partisi* (MSP)) was founded in October 1972. Like the MNP, which was closed in May 1971, the MSP fused Islam and Turkish nationalism. The MSP's slogan was "A Great Turkey Once Again" ("*Yeniden Büyük Türkiye*"). The party's proposed solution to Turkey's problems was to return to Islam's

---

[16] Barkey, "The Struggles of a 'Strong' State," p. 99.

[17] For background on the *Milli Görüş* movement and its philosophy, see Fulya Atacan, "Explaining Religious Politics at the Crossroad: AKP-SP," *Turkish Studies*, Vol. 6, No. 2, June 2005, pp. 187–199.

[18] See Ihsan D. Dağı, "Transformation of Islamic Political Identity in Turkey: Rethinking the West and Westernization," *Turkish Studies*, Vol. 6, No. 1, March 2005, pp. 21–37.

teachings and a "Muslim way of life." The MNP declared that the process of Westernization had fragmented Turkish society and led to a loss of grandeur and that a policy of industrialization, based on "native" heavy industry created by Anatolian capital, would create a strong nation that would turn its back on the West and become the leader of the Muslim world. In place of ties to the West, the MSP favored the creation of a Muslim Common Market, with the Islamic *dinar* as its common currency, and the development of a Muslim Defense Alliance.[19]

The MSP was a coalition of different Islamic and conservative groups. While the party's leader, Necmettin Erbakan, maintained tight political control, there were conflicts from the outset among the different groups and religious orders over the party's political orientation, as well as over Erbakan's authoritarian leadership style.[20] These political and ideological divisions became more pronounced after Erbakan's ill-fated tenure as prime minister (1996–1997) and eventually resulted in the split in the movement in 2001 that gave rise to the AKP.

In the 1970s, the MSP established itself as an important actor in Turkish political life. It gained third place in the 1973 election, with 12 percent of the vote and 11 percent of the seats in parliament. Erbakan formed a coalition government with the CHP, becoming deputy prime minister under Bülent Ecevit. After the coalition collapsed, the MSP joined the National Front governments headed by Süleyman Demirel in 1975 and 1977.

After the military coup in 1980, the MSP was closed down, and Erbakan and his lieutenants were banned from political activities for ten years. However, the party reemerged in 1983 under a new name— the Welfare Party (*Refah Partisi* (RP)). Welfare's ideology differed little from that of the MSP. It expressed the same hostility to Westernization

---

[19] On the MSP's program and ideology, see Jacob Landau, "The National Salvation Party in Turkey," *Asian and African Studies*, Vol. 11, 1976, pp. 1–57. Also Binnaz Toprak, "Politicization of Islam in a Secular State," in Said Arjomand (ed.), *From Nationalism to Revolutionary Islam*, London: Macmillan, 1984, pp. 119–133, and Binnaz Toprak, "Islam and Democracy in Turkey," *Turkish Studies*, Vol. 6, No. 2, June 2005, pp. 187–199.

[20] For a detailed discussion of the political and ideological struggles within the MSP, see Atacan, "Explaining Religious Politics at the Crossroad: AKP-SP," pp. 187–199.

and the same anti-Western bias. Its economic program, "Just Order," stressed the need for greater social justice and equality and an end to undue Western influence. In foreign policy, Welfare advocated cutting Turkey's ties to the West and closer integration with the Muslim world.

In the 1987 elections, Welfare received 7.16 percent of the vote—short of the 10 percent needed for representation in parliament. As a result, the religious right was not represented as a separate party in parliament during the 1980s. Many of Welfare's adherents joined Özal's Motherland Party (ANAP), which brought together religious and bureaucratic secular conservatives under one roof, siphoning off support from the religious right that otherwise would have gone to Welfare.

Political Islam in Power: The Welfare Interlude

Political Islam witnessed a strong resurgence in the early 1990s. In the March 1994 local elections, the Welfare Party received 19 percent of the vote and won the mayor's office in 28 municipalities, including Turkey's two largest cities, Istanbul and Ankara. In the 1995 national elections, Welfare came in first with 21.6 percent of the vote and formed a coalition with the right-of-center True Path Party (the successor to Demirel's Justice Party), with Erbakan as prime minister. Welfare's stunning victory sent shock waves throughout the secular establishment, especially the military. For the first time since the founding of the Turkish Republic in 1923, Turkey was run by an Islamist party, with an Islamist prime minister.

Several factors contributed to Welfare's strong showing. Perhaps most important was a shift in Welfare's political agenda, which put stronger emphasis on social issues rather than religious themes.[21] This allowed Welfare to broaden its appeal beyond the hard-core religious right. At the same time, Welfare's populist but catchy Just Order pro-

---

[21] Daği, "Transformation of Islamic Political Identity," p. 25.

gram allowed it to gain important support among the urban poor who traditionally had voted for the CHP.

Welfare was the best organized of all the political parties, with a legion of devout Muslims, especially women, who did volunteer work for the party and provided a network of social-welfare help to the poor. The party's grassroots network was extremely effective, working in the *gecekondu* and other poor urban areas, helping residents to find jobs, providing hospital and health care, distributing free food, and providing other social amenities.[22]

Welfare also benefited from a strong anti-Western backlash generated by the EU's rejection of Turkey's membership application at its December 1989 summit, which was seen by many Turks as motivated by cultural and religious biases, as well as by the West's failure to stop the killing of Muslims in Bosnia. The increasing disappointment with the West gave resonance to Welfare's strong anti-Western rhetoric.

However, once in office, Welfare showed little capacity for addressing Turkey's mounting domestic problems. Erbakan found it difficult to balance his anti-system campaign rhetoric with the need to consider the interests of the secular establishment, which was highly suspicious of his political goals, as well as of his commitment to democracy. Instead of pursuing policies designed to reduce social tensions, Erbakan further polarized Turkish society along secular-Islamic lines. He angered hard-core Islamist supporters by accepting a customs union with the EU and continuing to honor treaties with Israel that he had promised to annul. At the same time, he inflamed the secular establishment by saying that rectors of universities would have to kiss the hands of female students wearing headscarves (the wearing of headscarves was forbidden in universities) and threatening to build a mosque in Taksim Square, a major public transportation hub in the heart of Istanbul.[23]

---

[22] On Welfare's grassroots organization, see in particular Jenny B. White, *Islamic Mobilization in Turkey: A Study in Vernacular Politics*, Seattle and London: University of Washington Press, 2002. Also Yavuz, "Political Islam and the Welfare (Refah) Party in Turkey," pp. 71–73, and Toprak, "Islam and Democracy in Turkey," p. 181.

[23] The first Erdoğan-led municipal government of Istanbul tried to revive the Taksim Square mosque project, as well as another mosque project on the European side, in Göztepe Park. Both projects were shelved because of public opposition.

Moreover, in his first months in office, Erbakan undertook a number of foreign-policy initiatives—including an ill-fated trip to Libya and the promotion of an Islamic economic grouping (the D-8) as an alternative to the EU—that indicated that he intended to push an Islamist foreign policy.

These moves, together with Erbakan's often intemperate rhetoric, alarmed the secular establishment, particularly the military. However, rather than intervening directly, as it had in 1960, 1971, and 1980, the military used more-subtle and indirect methods to force Erbakan's ouster. On February 28, 1997, the National Security Council—which was dominated by the military—presented Erbakan with a list of recommendations to curb anti-secular activity.[24] When Erbakan balked at implementing the recommendations, the military held a series of briefings and mobilized the secular establishment against him, eventually forcing him to resign in June 1997 in what has been termed a "silent" or "post-modern" coup. In January 1998, the Welfare Party was closed down, and Erbakan and his key lieutenants were banned from politics for five years.

The Impact of the February 28 Process

The "February 28 process," as the military's effort to force Erbakan's resignation is termed in Turkey, was an important political watershed. It marked the abandonment of the idea that religion could be used to consolidate society, which had been at the root of the Turkish-Islamic synthesis. Thereafter, the military embarked on an overt campaign against Islamist ideas and ideology, which together with Kurdish separatism was singled out as one of the main threats to Turkish security.

At the same time, the February 28 process had an important impact on the orientation and development of the Islamist movement. It underscored the fact that a direct, head-on attempt to push an overt

---

[24] For the text of the military's February 28 recommendations in English and an analysis of the February 28 process and its aftermath, see Niyazi Gunay, "Implementing the 'February 28' Recommendations: A Scorecard," *Research Notes No. 10*, Washington Institute for Near East Policy, May 2001.

Islamic agenda could not succeed and would generate strong opposition from the secularists, especially the military. Many members of the Islamist movement concluded that the only way the Islamists could succeed was by avoiding a direct confrontation with the secularists and deemphasizing the religious agenda.

This recognition sparked an intense internal debate and rethinking within the Islamic movement about the movement's future political strategy and agenda, and a growing philosophical and political rift emerged within the movement between two different groups. The "traditionalists" (*Gelenekçiler*), centered on Erbakan and his chief lieutenant, Recai Kutan, opposed any serious change in approach or policy, while a younger group of "modernists," or "reformists" (*Yenilikçiler*), led by Recep Tayyip Erdoğan, the mayor of Istanbul, and his close associate Abdullah Gül, argued that the party needed to rethink its approach to a number of fundamental issues, particularly democracy, human rights, and relations with the West. The reformists also opposed Erbakan's authoritarian leadership style and called for greater inner-party democracy.

The influence of this internal debate was reflected in the platform of the Virtue Party (*Fazilet Partisi* (FP)), which replaced the Welfare Party. However, while Virtue was Welfare's successor, it differed in a number of important respects. Unlike Welfare, which was ideologically hostile to the West and Westernization, Virtue began to embrace Western political values. In short, anti-Westernism and suspicion of the West were no longer a hallmark of Islamist discourse.[25] A timeline of the religious-right parties is shown in Figure 3.1.

After the Virtue Party was shut down by the Constitutional Court in June 2001, the movement formally split. The traditionalists established the Felicity Party (*Saadet Partisi* (SP)), under the formal leadership of Recai Kutan, with Erbakan exerting the real leadership behind the scenes. The modernists founded a new party, the AKP, with Erdoğan

---

[25] This shift was symbolized by Virtue's decision to take Welfare's closure and Erbakan's ban from politics to the European Court of Human Rights (ECHR). As Ihsan Daği has noted, the decision to seek justice in Europe was particularly ironic in light of Erbakan's past stinging criticism of Europe as unjust, exploitative, and imperialistic. Daği, "Transformation of Islamic Political Identity," p. 28.

Figure 3.1
Evolution of Religious-Right Parties in Turkey

1950s	1960s	1970s	1980s	1990s	2000s
0 1 2 3 4 5 6 7 8 9	0 1 2 3 4 5 6 7 8 9	0 1 2 3 4 5 6 7 8 9	0 1 2 3 4 5 6 7 8 9	0 1 2 3 4 5 6 7 8 9	0 1 2 3 4 5 6 7

MNP · N P · SP

Active in center-right parties · I · MSP · RP · FP

AKP

	Erbakan and friends as independent MPs	**RP**	Refah Partisi (Welfare Party)
I	Erbakan and friends as independent MPs	**RP**	Refah Partisi (Welfare Party)
MNP	Milli Nizam Partisi (National Order Party)	**FP**	Fazilet Partisi (Virtue Party)
MSP	Milli Selamet Partisi (National Salvation Party)	**SP**	Saadet Partisi (Felicity Party)
N P	No political parties allowed by National Security Council	**AKP**	Adalet ve Kalkınma Partisi (Justice and Development Party)

RAND *MG726-3.1*

as party chairman. This split represented a fundamental ideological rift in the *Milli Görüş* movement. The older generation of politicians around Erbakan, who founded the Felicity Party, were traditionalists and adhered to many of the founding ideas of the movement. They saw their mission as establishing a "new civilization" based on traditional Islamic values and were reluctant to make practical compromises with the secular establishment to expand their political support.

They were also anti-Western and regarded Islam as incompatible with Western values. This anti-Westernism is a key feature of Felicity's political outlook and agenda. The party opposes Turkish membership in the EU, arguing that Turkey should intensify its ties to the Muslim world. Europe is portrayed as an enemy of Islam whose ultimate aim is to divide and weaken Turkey.

The founders of the AKP, by contrast, were open to cooperation with the secular establishment. The AKP program emphasizes the party's loyalty to the fundamental values and constitution of the Turkish Republic.[26] While the AKP has Islamic roots—many of its leaders,

---

[26] See *AK Parti Program* (AKP manifesto), August 14, 2001, p. 6, at http://eng.akparti.org.tr/english/partyprogramme.html (as of March 21, 2008).

including Erdoğan and Gül, came out of the *Milli Görüş* movement and had been members of the Welfare and Virtue parties—the AKP defines itself not as an Islamic party but as a conservative democratic party similar to Christian democratic parties in Western Europe.

This is an important ideological shift. Islamic political identity traditionally was built on opposition to the West, which was regarded as an entity to be rejected or countered. However, since its establishment in 2001, the AKP has increasingly emphasized Western political values such as democracy, respect for human rights, and the rule of law in its public discourse. At the same time, the party has come to view the West, especially the EU, as an important ally in its struggle against the restrictions of the Kemalist state. Whereas Islamists in Turkey in the past regarded Western calls for greater democratic reform as an attempt to impose alien values on Turkish society, the AKP sees the Western agenda increasingly overlapping with its own. The party views membership in the EU as a means of reducing the influence of the military and establishing a political framework that will expand religious tolerance and ensure its own political survival.

The jettisoning of anti-Western rhetoric has been accompanied by an abandonment of the anti-globalization discourse that characterized the Islamist movement in the past. The 2001 economic crisis made clear that strict adherence to the program of the International Monetary Fund (IMF) and attracting more foreign investment were indispensable to overcoming Turkey's financial difficulties and putting the Turkish economy back on its feet. Thus the AKP has promoted liberal market policies designed to attract foreign investment and integrate Turkey more closely into the global economy.

The Ascendency of the AKP

The AKP's ideological makeover and its adoption of a different political discourse have helped the party expand its political appeal and support. The AKP won the November 2002 elections with 34 percent of the vote, well ahead of the secularist CHP, which placed second with 19 percent of the vote. As only these two parties obtained sufficient votes to cross the 10 percent threshold needed for representation in parliament, the AKP received nearly two-thirds of the seats in the National Assembly, enabling it to form a government on its own.

The AKP's adoption of a more moderate and pragmatic political message undoubtedly contributed to its electoral success in the 2002 elections (see Figure 3.2). But several other factors helped as well. One was the disastrous performance of the Turkish economy. The Turkish currency was devalued several times, the banking sector was devastated, and the economy shrank by a historic 9.5 percent in 2001. A second contributing factor was corruption. The AKP was able to exploit public discontent with revelations of corruption in the mainstream secular parties and to portray itself as the party of "clean government."

The AKP also benefited from the demise of the Turkish left in the early 1990s. The AKP (and Welfare before it) succeeded in filling the vacuum created by the decline of the left, especially in working-class

Figure 3.2
Parliamentary-Election Performance of the Religious Right in Turkey

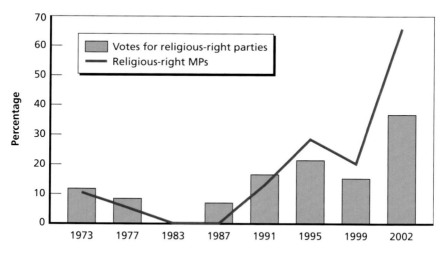

SOURCE: Turkstat, http://www.turkstat.gov.tr/PreIstatistikTablo.do?istab_id=199 for pre-1980 elections and http://www.turkstat.gov.tr/PreIstatistikTablo.do?istab_id=200 for 1980⊠2002 elections (as of March 21, 2008).

RAND MG726-3.2

neighborhoods. The AKP made its biggest gains among the recent immigrants in the *varoş*,[27] a group which today forms a plurality in Turkish urban areas. These people are pious and socially conservative and are not attracted to secular parties on either the left or the right.

The *varoş* is one of the most important sources of AKP power.[28] The AKP has skillfully drawn on its well-developed local infrastructure and social networks, much of which was established by the Welfare Party, to expand its political support among the working-class poor in Turkey's large urban areas. These factors, rather than an appeal to Islam, explain the AKP's success.

The July 22, 2007, Election

The results of the July 22, 2007, election demonstrate even more vividly the degree to which the AKP has been able to expand its base of support. Whereas it received 34 percent of the vote in the November 2002 election, it obtained 46.6 percent of the vote in the July 22, 2007, election—an increase of more than 12 percent. Moreover, the AKP increased its electoral support in all seven regions of the country. The most important increases occurred in the predominantly Kurdish areas of southeastern Anatolia. The AKP also increased its support in the five largest cities in Turkey. In Istanbul, it received almost as many votes as all its opponents combined. This suggests that the AKP is gradually extending its hold from the periphery toward the city centers. The party's main support, however, comes from the poorer and less-developed parts of the cities (the *varoş*).

While the 2007 election showed clear cleavages between the center and the periphery, with the CHP doing best in the wealthier parts of the larger cities, it also showed, as Tanju Tosun has pointed out, that the AKP represents a catch-all party and should not be regarded

---

[27] Lower-class residential areas on the outskirts of urban centers.

[28] On the importance of the *varoş* in AKP's 2002 electoral victory, see Soner Cagaptay, "Secularism and Foreign Policy in Turkey," The Washington Institute for Near East Policy, Policy Focus #67, April 2007, pp. 26 and 34.

as a religious party.[29] Indeed, the support it received from different social groups gives the AKP the attributes of a center-right party. It has managed to blend cultural preferences typical of the right with social-economic policies that are generally associated with the left and that are favored by the electorate as a whole.[30] Economic stability was a primary concern of the voters and a key factor in the AKP's electoral success. The military's so-called "midnight memorandum" on April 27, 2007, which contained a veiled threat of possible military intervention, also seems to have contributed to the increase in the AKP's popular support.

---

[29] Tanju Tosun, "The July 22 Elections: A Chart for the Future of Turkish Politics," *Private View*, No. 12, Autumn 2007, p. 54.

[30] Ibid, p. 56.

CHAPTER FOUR

The AKP in Power

Despite the AKP's claim of being a conservative democratic party, many Turkish secularists and outside observers still question whether it has abandoned the Islamist agenda of its predecessors and reconciled itself to operating within the framework of Turkish secularism, or whether the priority that the party has given to privatization, structural reforms, and integration with the EU over a religious agenda merely represents a tactical shift in its political strategy. This chapter reviews the AKP's record in power in an attempt to assess the validity of these concerns.

The Reconfiguration of Turkish Politics

After the AKP won the November 2002 elections, Erdoğan declared that his priority was economic stability and EU membership, and he downplayed the social issues at the core of the Islamist agenda. Despite its Islamist roots, the AKP realized the advantages of speaking the language of modernity and of integration with Europe. The EU membership project was supported by business circles and the public at large, and the emphasis on democracy and human rights enabled the AKP to attempt to curb the influence of the military in politics and to chip away at the entrenched Kemalist establishment.[1]

---

[1] Some of the most important reforms preceded the AKP's accession to power. The constitutional amendment that changed the composition of the National Security Council to reflect greater civilian influence was approved in October 2001 as part of an EU-oriented reform

The reorientation of the AKP toward Europe contributed to the reconfiguration of Turkish politics. As the West became a tacit ally of the AKP, formerly pro-Western secularists surfaced as opponents of EU accession. The CHP, once the champion of a Western orientation for Turkey, has increasingly moved in a more nationalistic direction and has adopted a more ambiguous attitude toward the West, seeing some aspects of the West's influence as a threat to the integrity of the Turkish state and Kemalism.

As discussed in the preceding chapter, the emergence of the AKP as the dominant political party in Turkey is associated with the emergence of new economic and social forces in Turkish society. The new social sector—the religious entrepreneurial class—developed after Turgut Özal inaugurated the privatization process of the 1980s and mushroomed in Anatolia. Its members were small and medium-sized entrepreneurs from rural or small-town backgrounds, most of whom were based in Istanbul. In one view of Turkish political dynamics, the religious-secularist divide in Turkish society reflects the redistribution of power from the traditional business establishment and its allies in the bureaucracy and the military to this rising social sector, which finds political expression in the AKP.

The religious business sector is represented by MÜSİAD (Independent Industrialists' and Businessmen's Association),[2] founded in 1990 as an alternative to TÜSİAD (Turkish Industrialists' and Businessmen's Association), which represents Turkey's business establishment. Although many of its leaders are close to the AKP, MÜSİAD professes not to be a political organization. It has a social as well as an economic agenda, and it wants to expand the freedom of individuals to engage in religiously oriented activities in the workplace and to

---

package. Similarly, the death penalty was abolished in two stages, in October 2001 and August 2002, before the AKP took power. "Turkish Constitution," at http://www.tbmm. gov.tr/Anayasa.htm (as of March 21, 2008); "2002 Progress Report on Turkey's EU Accession Process," 2002, at http://www.abgs.gov.tr/files/AB_Iliskileri/AdaylikSureci/Ilerleme Raporlari/Turkiye_Ilerleme_Rap_2002.pdf (as of March 21, 2008).

[2] While the association's name starts with *Müstakil* (independent or unaffiliated), it is widely believed that the word is a placeholder for *Müslüman*, i.e., Muslim.

end discrimination against religious Muslims. It also seeks to translate Islamic values into business practice and social policy.[3]

MÜSİAD publishes *Çerçeve,* a quarterly trade journal for members. In the March 2006 issue, the letter from the association's president states: "Our great religion of Islam dictates that nine tenths of earning is in trade, and declares that interest is unlawful *[haram],* but that legitimate trade and profit are lawful *[helal].*" The letter also states that "shopping centers bigger than 3,000 square meters must be required to have some appropriate space for prayers." Another article in the same issue starts with, "The main idea of the Western-origin consumption economy is that you count as much as you consume. Of course, this is a trap; one must be wary."[4]

Also worth noting is TUSKON (Confederation of Businessmen and Industrialists of Turkey), a recently established organization that explicitly represents the interests of conservative Anatolian entrepreneurs in Turkey and abroad. TUSKON was founded in Istanbul in 2005 and expanded throughout the country and abroad. It opened an office in Washington, D.C., in October 2007.[5] TUSKON does not have an overt political agenda, but its founders and members are close to the Gülen movement. (TUSKON is considered to be the "fourth leg" of the movement, the other three being its education, media, and interfaith dialogue activities.)

The AKP: A New Synthesis or Islamism in Disguise?

The reconfiguration of Turkish politics in the AKP's first five years in office raises the question of whether the AKP represents a new synthesis in Turkish politics. AKP officials argue that the AKP does not have an Islamist agenda. The party, İhsan Dağı argues, represents peripheral Islamic social and cultural conservatism, but it is pursuing a modern-

---

[3] Interview with MÜSİAD officials, Istanbul, June 2007.

[4] Tüketirken Tükenmek, *Çerçeve,* Nissan 2007, at http://www.musiad.org.tr/yayinlarRaporlar/detay.asp?yayinRapor=46&k=1 (as of March 21, 2008).

[5] See the TUSKON web site at www.tuskon.org.

izing agenda.[6] The important thing, according to an AKP official, is not *whether* Islam influences politics, but *how* it influences politics. A liberal interpretation of Islam, he says, can influence politics in a liberal way.[7]

The public positions and policies of the AKP government are a sharp departure from the political Islam represented by Erbakan. As prime minister in the Welfare Party–led government in 1996–1997, Erbakan indulged in a polarizing Islamist rhetoric; internationally, he attempted to create an Islamic bloc. On establishing the AKP, Erdoğan explicitly stated that the party was not going to be an Islamist party and that the party members were simply "Muslim democrats." He made Turkey's accession to the EU a central part of his program and, with the exception of the 2004 adultery-law fiasco (see below), has generally distanced the party from divisive social issues. Alevi AKP Member of Parliament Reha Çamuroğlu argues that all of the AKP positions can be defined in secular terms. Islamic politics, he says, has no future.[8]

Internally, the party leadership's decision to replace about 200 candidates identified with the more-religious wing of the party on its July 2007 electoral list (some of the new candidates come from the liberal and center-left sectors of Turkish politics) has been portrayed as intended to distance the party from old-line Islamist elements.[9]

Secularists argue that because of the potency of political Islam, only a "hard" secularism could prevent it from overwhelming Turkey's political institutions. There is a widespread belief among secularists that the AKP's moderate public posture is window dressing and that the party has changed its tactics, but not its strategy. Critics cite hard-line statements by party leaders in the 1990s as indications of the AKP's true agenda—for example, Abdullah Gül's statement on the eve of the 1996 parliamentary election that "this is the end of the repub-

---

[6] Daği, 2007.

[7] Discussion with a senior AKP official, Istanbul, June 2007.

[8] Interview with Reha Çamuroğlu, Istanbul, June 2007.

[9] Of those replaced, 165 were removed outright and 40 were placed in non-electable positions on the AKP list. Interview with Suat Kınıklıoğlu, former Director of the Marshall Fund of the United States in Ankara and current AKP member of parliament, Ankara, June 2007.

lican period,"[10] or Erdoğan's statements in 1996 that democracy is not an end, but only a means, and that as mayor of Istanbul, he was "a servant of *shari'a*" and the "imam of Istanbul."[11]

A failed attempt by the Erdoğan government to criminalize adultery in 2004 also fueled secularists' fears that underneath the AKP's veneer of modernity there is an Islamist core. Ironically, the adultery provision was part of the reform of the Turkish penal code (TCK) that the government undertook to meet European conditions for starting the talks on accession to the EU. The attempt to introduce an adultery clause into the penal code reform package predictably generated a strong reaction by the secularist opposition, as well as by the Europeans. Abdullah Gül, Erdoğan's point man on EU accession, pledged to the CHP that the AKP would not act unilaterally to pass the adultery legislation and that amendments to the penal code would be co-sponsored by the two parties. But according to Turkish press reports, Erdoğan came under pressure from conservatives in the AKP and pressed ahead with the adultery law. When it became clear that such legislation, imposed through the majority AKP vote in parliament, could provoke a serious political crisis as well as sour relations with the EU, the government withdrew the TCK reform bill.[12]

Of great concern to secularists are what they consider to be AKP efforts to Islamize the educational system and the judiciary—two strongholds of Turkish secularism. A major controversy developed over the question of whether graduates of *Imam Hatip* religious schools should be able to enter non-religious faculties in universities (AKP supporters argue that it is a matter of removing discrimination, discussed below). The government has been accused of taking a permissive approach toward illegal Quran schools and of seeking to introduce an Islamic agenda into higher-education policy. Related legislation low-

---

[10] "Turkish Islamists aim for power," *The Guardian* (London), November 27, 1995.

[11] Chart of statements by Virtue Party leaders on social issues, cited in Seda Demiralp and Todd A. Eisenstadt, *Prisoner Erdoğan's Dilemma and the Origins of Moderate Islam in Turkey*, Washington, D.C.: American University, Department of Government, August 31, 2006.

[12] Yusuf Kanlı, "Confidence crisis between Erdoğan and EU," *Turkish Daily News*, September 20, 2004.

ered the mandatory retirement age of government employees, which would, in theory, replace more than 2,000 officials.[13]

From the AKP perspective, some sectors of the judiciary use their authority to block legislation and undermine the AKP; for example, in June 2005, the chief prosecutor of the Supreme Court of Appeals identified eight AKP bylaws that contravened Turkish law and asked for censure of the party.[14] The Constitutional Court decision that blocked the first attempt to elect Abdullah Gül as president is also considered by many Turkish and outside observers as having been politically motivated. (Gül was eventually elected president on August 28, 2007.)

Şerif Mardin, one of Turkey's most respected scholars of Ottoman and Turkish history, notes that the AKP is the fifth avatar of an Islamic discourse that has been evolving since the 1890s and that it is difficult to say where it stands today. The AKP has learned the rules of democratic politics that require compromise. But, Mardin asks, how many layers of a clientele does it have and where do these layers come from? He notes that these layers have been little studied but must be understood to evaluate the AKP's political agenda. AKP leaders are not theoreticians of Islam. They are not interested in ideology. What they are interested in is promoting "everyday Islam": taxes on alcohol, or looking the other way when someone in a school distributes literature that celebrates the Prophet's birthday. It is not a question of the state imposing an Islamic agenda, but of spontaneous actions by lower-level officials who believe that it is part of their mission. It is a dynamic phenomenon with possibilities that cannot be predicted.[15]

---

[13] A 2003 *Hürriyet* article reports the number of officials to be replaced at 2,100 across all departments and agencies of government. Süleyman Demirkan, "Çiğdem Toker, 61 yaşında emeklilik telaşı," *Hürriyet*, March 18, 2003. The parliament passed the related bill in March 2003, but the president returned it for reconsideration. It was passed again with no change in April 2003, but upon the application of the CHP, the Constitutional Court ordered a stay of it in May 2003. The parliament passed a slightly revised bill for the same cause in July 2003. The CHP again took the matter to court, and the Constitutional Court again ordered a stay and annulled the law in October 2003. Oya Armutçu, "61 yaşında emekliliğe iptal," *Hürriyet*, October 9, 2003.

[14] Michael Rubin, "Will Turkey Have an Islamist President?" *Middle Eastern Outlook*, American Enterprise Institute for Foreign Policy Research, No. 1, February 2007, at http://www.meforum.org/article/1637.

[15] Interview with Şerif Mardin, Istanbul, June 2007.

"Green Money"

An issue that has generated a great deal of controversy in Turkey relates to companies with Islamist owners that went public without registering with financial authorities and collected large amounts of money from Turks in Germany, many of whom lost their investment. Most of these holding companies ("green holdings") were based in Konya, the cradle of Turkish Islamism, and their operations coincided with the rise of the Welfare Party. (Of the 78 green holdings examined by the Turkish parliamentary commission, 55 are based in Konya province.) The management of Yimpaş Holding, one of the leading green holdings, confessed to a bankruptcy court in Germany that its German subsidiary sent DEM 20 million to a Turkish party in 1999.[16] Although German authorities did not disclose the party's identity, there would be little reason to expect that it would be any other than the Virtue Party.

Under Turkish capital-markets law, before a company can offer its shares or bonds to the public, it has to register with the Capital Markets Board (CMB), a procedure that is substantially identical to U.S. capital-markets regulations. Along with the rise of the religious right, a large number of green holdings were founded with the purpose of raising money ("green capital") from devout believers in Turkey and Germany. Such companies ignored registration requirements. Funds would be collected from investors in exchange for receipts or purported share certificates (which have no formal value), and the money would be delivered to Turkey by special couriers.[17] Yimpaş Holding and Kombassan Holding, founded in 1982 and 1985, respectively, were the pioneers of the green-capital phenomenon. More such companies were established in the 1990s, and the industry boomed between 1997 and 1999.[18]

---

[16] "20 milyon mark hangi siyasi partiye gitti?" *Radikal*, November 4, 2006.

[17] Adnan Keskin, "Endüstri' davası emsal oluyor, yeşil şirketlere 'çete' kıskacı," *Radikal*, January 31, 2007.

[18] Zihni Erdem and Ahmet Kıvanç, "Gurbetçi parası RP ve FP'ye," *Radikal*, December 16, 2005.

In the late 1990s, CMB investigated a total of 77 such holding companies that were known to have raised money without registering. These investigations have produced mixed results, as most of the capital was raised off the books, and Turkish courts were not very experienced with capital-markets fraud. However, at least the two pioneers have been subject to prosecution. In June 2007, the Turkish Supreme Court affirmed a two-year prison term for the chairman and ten board members of Yimpaş. In the same month, the Court also overturned the judgment of a Konya court that had released the board of directors of Kombassan on identical charges.[19]

After the election of the AKP government in 2002, the opposition CHP began to raise the issue of green holdings in parliament. In March 2005, a commission was set up to investigate the matter. The commission's 270-page report was discussed and approved by parliament in April 2006. Among other findings, the report concludes that at least €5 billion were collected by green holdings. The parliament-endorsed report was forwarded to the Prime Ministry and the Ministry of Justice, but no action has been taken to date.[20]

It was also recently revealed that Deniz Feneri e.V., the Germany-based European branch of Turkish charity Deniz Feneri Derneği (DFD), has engaged in dubious financial operations, along with sister enterprise TV Channel 7. This organization dates back to 1996, when small-scale and temporary charity activities were showcased as part of the *"Şehir ve Ramazan"* ("Ramadan and the City") program on Channel 7.[21] Catching the popular imagination, the show became permanent under the name *"Deniz Feneri"* ("Lighthouse"). In 1998, DFD was registered as a charitable association in Istanbul, i.e., a separate organi-

---

[19] "Kombassan ve Yimpaş'ta şok," *Radikal*, June 16, 2007.

[20] It has been alleged that green-holding influence within the AKP is the reason the government has avoided addressing the issue of illegal activities by these entities. The chairman of Yimpaş Holding, one of the leading green holdings, categorically denies allegations that his enterprise was allocated parliament members in exchange for hefty donations, while acknowledging that "a few friends working for him have become mayors, MPs, and ministers." "Komisyon önerdi: Hükümet dinlemedi," *Radikal*, November 1, 2006.

[21] Biz Kimiz, Deniz Feneri Derneği, at http://www.denizfeneri.org.tr/icerik.asp?kategori= KURUMSAL.

zation. Quickly expanding and opening offices in Ankara and Izmir (in 2000 and 2002, respectively), it was granted tax-exempt status in 2004.[22] The European division, DFE, states that it aims to organize charitable activities by Turks living in Germany and elsewhere.[23]

In April 2007, on the basis of suspected money-laundering activity, Frankfurt authorities raided the offices of DFE and collocated Channel 7 Europe, concluding a one-and-a-half-year investigation. The financial police also combed the residences of fourteen DFE and Channel 7 personnel and arrested the head of Channel 7 Europe and an officer of DFE.[24] Of €14 million in donations raised by DFE between 2002 and 2006 Europe-wide, €8 million is alleged to have been diverted to Channel 7 for unknown purposes.[25] German authorities have also determined the identities of five couriers in charge of moving cash around and uncovered links between DFE and several commercial organizations based in Turkey and Germany, including a marketing company that focuses on Islamic publications and a seaside resort near Izmir.[26] The Turkish daily *Hürriyet* reports DFD as having declared an annual fundraising capacity of $100 million.[27] DFD also serves as the secretariat of the Humanitarian Help Forum of the Organization of the Islamic Conference.[28] DFD's position is that it has no organic link with DFE.

There have also been allegations that the AKP has received money from the Middle East. Michael Rubin, who has looked at the issue of green money in Turkey, says that there has been an opaque influx of Islamist capital under AKP management of the economy, but the evi-

---

[22] "Beş İslami derneğin yükselişi," *Radikal*, April 27, 2007

[23] Biz Kimiz, Deniz Feneri e.V., op. cit.

[24] İsmail Erel, "Kanal 7 müdürü tutuklandı 8 milyon Euro aranıyor," *Hürriyet*, April 27, 2007.

[25] "Alman polisinden Kanal 7 INT'e baskın," *Radikal*, April 26, 2007.

[26] "Deniz Feneri'nin kuryeleri belirlendi," *Hürriyet*, June 18, 2007.

[27] Serkan Akkoç, "Almanya'da Kanal 7 ve Deniz Feneri'ne kara para baskını," *Hürriyet*, April 26, 2007.

[28] "İnsani yardım kuruluşları tek çatı altında birleşecek," *Hürriyet*, February 24, 2007.

dence is inconclusive.[29] (It should be noted that the problem of unregulated cash investments is not confined to businesses with Islamic connections.)

Although there is no hard evidence of Middle East funding of the AKP, there appear to be linkages between the party and the Islamic financial sector. Executives associated with the Islamic banking sector have been appointed to state financial institutions. For example, a large part of the management cadre of Ülker's Islamic finance institutions was transferred to manage the two large state banks after the AKP took over. In May 2006, Erdoğan tried to appoint a specialist in Islamic finance as governor of the Central Bank, but his candidate was rejected by the president.[30] The secularists are concerned that the AKP is trying to infiltrate Islamists into key positions in the Central Bank. However, given the ideological divide in Turkey, any high-profile appointment by the AKP is likely to become politicized.

The Headscarf Controversy

The headscarf has become an enormously important symbol in the debate in Turkey on the role of religion and the state, but it is not a high-priority issue for most people. Only 3.7 percent of the respon-

---

[29] Rubin cites Ilhan Kesici, former under secretary at the State Planning Organization, who says that much of the money enters the country in suitcases and remains outside regulation. Rubin points out that in Erdoğan's first year in office, the net error in the balance of payments rose from $118 million to $4.9 billion and has again approached record levels; he suggests that much of this unexplained influx of capital comes from Middle Eastern sources. This could be right, of course, but errors in the balance of payments are unexplained by definition and could be due to a variety of factors, including bad estimates. The Central Bank of Turkey published a special report on this issue, elaborating on the net error and omission (NEO) item. See "An Evaluation Related to the Net Error and Omission Item in the Balance of Payments," November 2005, at http://www.tcmb.gov.tr/yeni/evds/yayin/kitaplar/Net%20Hata%20ve%20Noksan.pdf (as of March 21, 2008).

[30] The government's candidate was Adnan Büyükdeniz, an executive officer of the Islamic finance group AlBaraka Türk. President Sezer vetoed the nomination as an "inappropriate" choice. Andrew Birch, "Turkey: The Search for a New Central Bank Governor," *Global Insight*, at http://www.globalinsight.com/Perspective/PerspectiveDetail2936.htm.

dents to the 2006 TESEV study chose the headscarf as the issue most important to them.[31] For AKP supporters, wearing the headscarf is a matter of personal choice, and restrictions on its use are violations of individual rights. As a practical matter, the ban on the headscarf presents young religious women with the choice of removing the scarf (and violating their religious obligation or convictions) or not being able to attend a public university or enter an official space.[32]

The point, in the AKP view, is that people should be able to express their Islamic identity in state institutions.[33] According to an AKP member of parliament, the party makes a distinction between state employees and ordinary citizens. Under the current dress code, state employees cannot and should not wear the headscarf, but consumers of state services are not so constrained. What is needed, he says, is a social consensus that works for everyone.[34]

For secularists, the use of the headscarf in public spaces represents less a personal choice than a political attack on the fabric of the secular state. They view the headscarf as a ubiquitous and visible symbol of the Islamization of Turkish society that they fear. Of the 22 percent of the respondents to the 2006 TESEV survey who believed that secularism was under threat (72 percent disagreed), the overwhelming majority cited the headscarf as a sign of this threat. Secular women are very sensitive to this issue.[35]

In this regard, there is an apparent disconnect between perception and reality. According to the 2006 TESEV survey, 64 percent of the respondents believed that the use of the headscarf has increased in recent years, but the reality, according to TESEV, is that use actually

---

[31] Çarkoğlu and Toprak, 2006, p. 45.

[32] However, according to the 2006 TESEV study, 65 percent of the fathers in the poll would let their daughters remove their headscarves if this was the stipulation for entering a university.

[33] Discussion with a senior AKP official, Istanbul, June 2007.

[34] Interview with Suat Kınıklıoğlu, Ankara, June 2007.

[35] Çarkoğlu and Toprak, 2006, pp. 58–59.

decreased between 1999 and 2006.[36] The reason for the gap between perception and reality may be that headscarf-wearing women are now present in greater numbers in the marketplace and in urban venues from which they were previously absent.

The profile of the headscarf issue was raised considerably by the controversy over the participation of the headscarf-wearing spouses of Prime Minister Erdoğan and other AKP leaders in official events.[37] President Sezer enforced a ban on the headscarf from events at the Presidential Palace. (Most of the invitations from Sezer did not include headscarf-wearing spouses. While some AKP figures complied with this, others refused to attend in protest.)

One of the major secularist objections to Gül's presidential candidacy was that his wife wears a headscarf. For this reason, his election to the presidency by the AKP is likely to remain a source of strain between the AKP government and the secularists. Before the July 2007 election, the AKP posture on the headscarf was circumspect; its wearing by the wives of AKP leaders signaled to the rank and file the leadership's commitment to Islamic values, but the party did not directly challenge the ban.

However, the AKP's overwhelming victory in the July 22, 2007, elections appears to have emboldened the Erdoğan government to try to get the headscarf ban lifted for women attending universities. In February 2008, parliament amended two articles of the constitution in order to create the constitutional framework for the lifting of the ban in universities.[38] Based on the amendments, the head of the Higher

---

[36] According to the TESEV survey, the use of the different types of headscarf has decreased as follows from 1999 to 2006: (1) *başörtüsü* (the classical headscarf), 53.4 percent to 48.8 percent; (2) *türban* (the type of headscarf that covers the hair, neck, and shoulders), 15.7 percent to 11.4 percent; (3) *çarşaf* (full covering), 3.4 percent to 1.1 percent. The proportion of women not wearing the scarf increased from 27.3 percent to 36.5 percent. Çarkoğlu and Toprak, 2006, pp. 58–59.

[37] The constitution bans displays of religious symbols in official places.

[38] Article 10, on Equality Before the Law, was amended by adding to its last sentence, ". . . and in benefitting from all public services." Article 42, on Right and Duty of Training and Education, was amended by adding the statement, "No one can be deprived of the right to receive higher education for reasons not openly mentioned by laws. The limits of the use

Education Council (YÖK), an AKP appointee, instructed all universities in the country to start admitting students wearing headscarves, with immediate effect. However, only about a dozen of Turkey's 115 universities appear to have complied. The resistance to lifting the ban by many university authorities suggests that the ban is likely to remain a source of tension between the AKP and the secularists.

The *Imam-Hatip* Schools Controversy

Another controversial issue is whether the selection system used for university entrance that discriminates against graduates of *İmam-Hatip* schools should be abandoned. The YÖK rendered a decision in 1997 that secondary-school graduates who took the university entrance examination would earn higher scores if they applied for programs that coincided with the type of secondary school they attended. This meant that *İmam-Hatip* school graduates would receive the higher scores only if they applied for admission to faculties of theology. To compete for entrance to non-theology faculties, *İmam-Hatip* school graduates would have to achieve higher scores than graduates of other schools.

As large numbers of *İmam-Hatip* school graduates began to enter the universities as public administration and law majors in the 1990s, the *İmam-Hatip* schools issue became a point of friction between the Erbakan government and the military. The decision to restrict the admission of *İmam-Hatip* graduates to non-theology faculties reflected the secularists' fears that the schools had ceased to be vocational schools for the training of clergymen and had become an alternative to the national education system.[39] However, religious Turks regard the

---

of this right will be determined by law." "Amendment does not free headscarf," *Newstime7*, March 9, 2008, at http://www.newstime7.com/haber/20080309/Amendment-does-not-free-headscarf.php (as of March 21, 2008).

[39] Bahattin Akşit, cited in Henry Rutz, "The Rise and Demise of *İmam-Hatip* Schools: Discourses of Islamic Belonging and Denial in the Construction of Turkish Civil Culture," *PoLAR: Political and Legal Anthropology Review*, Vol. 22, No. 2, November 1999, at http://www.anthrosource.net/doi/abs/10.1525/pol.1999.22.2.93 (as of March 21, 2008). The secularist argument is that *İmam-Hatip* schools are vocational schools under the current educational system. They are intended to produce imams as a well-defined profession, just as

İmam-Hatip schools primarily as a vehicle for their children to receive a religious education, not necessarily as vocational schools.

The AKP government has been looking for ways to allow *İmam-Hatip* school graduates to receive preferential treatment in gaining admission to non-theology faculties, for instance, by allowing them to transfer to regular state schools before graduation.[40] In December 2005, the Ministry of Education issued a regulation allowing *İmam-Hatip* students to earn degrees from regular high schools by taking correspondence courses. However, the YÖK objected, and in February 2006, the Council of State suspended the regulation pending a final ruling.[41] Secularists framed the issue as the penetration of the state bureaucracy by Islamists, while AKP supporters put it in terms of removing discrimination against *İmam-Hatip* school graduates. The latter appears to be the majority view among the population at large. According to the 2006 TESEV study, 82 percent of the respondents believe that *İmam-Hatip* graduates should have a level playing field for university entrance.[42]

---

technical high schools are supposed to produce technicians. If graduates of technical schools want to attend the engineering department of a university, they have an advantage over non-technical graduates, but they are at a disadvantage if they apply for admission to non-technical departments. Similarly, *İmam-Hatip* school graduates have an advantage over others when they apply for admission to theological faculties, but they are at a disadvantage if they apply to other departments. From the secularist point of view, what the AKP is trying to do is redefine the role of the *İmam-Hatip* schools as a step in the direction of an Islamic state where mastering the Quran would be the norm and not part of a specialized professional education.

[40] Soner Cagaptay, "How Will the Turkish Military React?" Madrid: Real Instituto Elcano, July 16, 2007.

[41] U.S. Department of State, "Turkey: International Religious Freedom Report 2006," at http://www.state.gov/g/drl/rls/irf/2006/71413.htm (as of March 21, 2008).

[42] Çarkoğlu and Toprak, 2006, p. 5.

Non-Muslim Minorities Under AKP Rule

Non-Muslim minorities—primarily the Greek, Armenian, and Jewish communities—view the AKP ascendancy with mixed feelings. On one hand, some members of these communities share the secularists' fear that the AKP's long-term agenda may be to create some form of an Islamic state in Turkey. Although the Kemalist state has been as restrictive of other religions as it has been of Islam, some non-Muslims believe that they are better off under a secular state than they would be under a more Islam-oriented state.[43]

Concerns about the AKP's religious orientation and the Islamization of society appear to be most prevalent among members of the Jewish community. This may be because anti-Semitism in Turkey is seen as an Islamist theme. The majority of the respondents in a 2006 study of perceptions of anti-Semitism among Turkish Jews said they believed that Turkish society was not very fertile ground for anti-Semitism, but that anti-Semitism was being imported from abroad.[44] Jewish stereotypes are prevalent, however. Among the respondents to the 2006 TESEV report, 55 percent think Jews manage the world economy, and 53 percent think influential circles in Turkey serve Jewish interests.[45]

Islamists rely on two issues to spread anti-Semitism: the Israeli-Palestinian conflict—and the conflation of anti-Zionism with anti-Semitism—and religious themes associated with the rise of radical

---

[43] Soner Cagaptay stated that in a visit to Midyat, a Syriac community leader told him that before the AKP came to power, government authorities were helpful in facilitating the return of Syriacs who had been driven out of their homes by the PKK, but AKP-appointed authorities have a negative attitude and are reluctant to provide services to Christians. Soner Cagaptay, "Turkish Troubles," *The Wall Street Journal Europe*, July 30, 2007, at http://online.wsj.com/public/article/SB118574382583581533.htm (as of March 21, 2008).

[44] Jewish stereotypes and conspiracy theories are pervasive, but anti-Semitism, defined as hatred of Jews, is seen as not widespread and not part of any official policy. See Şule Toktaş, "Perceptions of Anti-Semitism Among Turkish Jews," *Turkish Studies*, Vol. 7, No. 2, June 2006, p. 211.

[45] Çarkoğlu and Toprak, 2006, p. 80.

Islam.[46] Because of its distrust of Islamism, the Jewish community appears to have backed the CHP in the July 2007 elections, despite the fact that the party had grown increasingly hostile to the West over the previous several years and has a poor record on minority rights.

Anti-Semitism is not restricted to Islamists; it is equally, if not more, prevalent in ultranationalist circles. One of Turkey's best sellers is a book by a Kemalist author, Ergün Poyraz, entitled *Children of Moses*. The book argues that Erdoğan and his wife are "crypto-Jews" who are conspiring with the Mossad to destroy secularism in Turkey. Poyraz has also written two other books, *The Gül of Moses* and *The Mujahid of Moses*, in which he claims that then Foreign Minister Abdullah Gül and Parliament Speaker Bülent Arınç are also secret Jews who serve the Elders of Zion and threaten Turkey's secular republic.[47]

The AKP's agenda of opening space for religion in society could increase the ability of non-Muslim religious communities to operate more freely. For example, legislation introduced by the first AKP government would have liberalized the strict rules governing minority-run foundations and would have created a mechanism for returning minority property confiscated by the state. The bill was strongly opposed by CHP members of parliament. Relaxation of restrictions on religious training could also be to the advantage of Christian denominations. The new AKP government is more likely to approve the opening of the Greek Orthodox Halkı seminary—the subject of a chronic dispute between the patriarchate and the Turkish government—than a government dominated by nationalists would be.[48]

---

[46] The perpetrators of the Neva Shalom synagogue bombing in Istanbul in November 2003 were part of al-Qaeda's global jihadist network.

[47] Mustafa Akyol, "Meet Turkey's real Islamists," *Turkish Daily News*," July 19, 2007, at http://www.turkishdailynews.com.tr/article.php?enewsid=78690 (as of March 21, 2008).

[48] The authors were told by a senior AKP official in June 2007 that Abdullah Gül favors approving the opening of the seminary. The issue is very complex, because it goes to the heart of state-religion relations in Turkey. The argument against allowing it to be opened is that if the state allowed the Greek Orthodox Church to open the seminary, Muslims would demand the same right. The authorities are said to be willing to allow the seminary to open under the faculty of theology of the University of Istanbul, but that would take the seminary out of the patriarchate's control.

Agos, the Armenian weekly, estimated before the July 2007 elections that nearly 60 percent of Turkey's 70,000 Armenians would vote for the AKP. Michail Vasiliadis, editor of *Apoyevmatini,* a Greek-language daily newspaper published in Istanbul, says he believes Turkey's ethnic Greek community, estimated at 2,000 people, was also backing the AKP.[49] A dramatic manifestation of the more nuanced attitude of Christian minorities toward the AKP was the support for the AKP of the Armenian patriarch, Mesrob II Mutafyan. Speaking to the German weekly *Der Spiegel,* the patriarch claimed the Armenian community would prefer the AKP to the CHP because the AKP's approach to minorities is coherent and less nationalistic.[50]

The AKP and the Kurds

The AKP has also made important inroads among the Kurds. In the July 22, 2007, elections, the AKP doubled its vote from eastern and southeastern cities that traditionally voted for pro-Kurdish parties (54 percent in 2007 vs. 27.29 percent in 2002). One reason for the AKP's success appears to be its more open and tolerant approach to the Kurdish issue. However, the influence of religious groups, particularly the Nakşibendi Sufi order, also appears to have played a role.[51] The Nakşibendi, which is the best organized Islamic group in the Kurdish region, has criticized the predominantly Kurdish Democratic Society Party (*Demokratik Toplum Partisi* (DTP)) quite harshly, and this criticism, according to some observers, has begun to have an impact on the party's base. Contrary to the claims of the DTP, which contends

---

[49] "Turkey: Religious Minorities Watch Closely as Election Day Approaches," Eurasianet, July 19, 2007, at http://www.eurasianet.org/departments/insight/articles/eav071907a.shtml (as of March 21, 2008).

[50] "Veteran diplomat, Armenian patriarch lend support to AKP," *Turkish Daily News,* June 5, 2007, at http://www.turkishdailynews.com.tr/article.php?enewsid=75000 (as of March 21, 2008).

[51] See Bahadır Özgür, "The Naqshi Kurdish Opposition Hit the DTP Where It Hurts," *Turkish Daily News,* August 6, 2007, at http://www.turkishdailynews.com.tr/article.php?enewsid=80163 (as of March 21, 2008).

that the influence of sects in the Kurdish regions has declined in recent years, their influence among the Kurds appears to have increased.

At the same time, the DTP has come under strong criticism for the refusal of its representatives in parliament to condemn PKK terrorism and for the party's alleged ties to the PKK. In fall 2007, the public prosecutor's office petitioned the Constitutional Court to ban the DTP because of its attitude toward the PKK and its support for autonomy of the Kurdish regions in Turkey. The petition has presented a dilemma for the AKP: The Erdoğan government does not want to be perceived as being soft on terrorism at a time when the PKK has stepped up its terrorist attacks, but it is hesitant to support a ban on political parties, since this could set a precedent that could be used by the Kemalists to legitimize banning the AKP.

The AKP and the Military

The military, the chief avatars and defenders of Kemalism, and the AKP, a party with Islamist roots, coexist within the framework of Turkish democracy, but at bottom, there is a tension between each side's strategic objectives vis-à-vis those of the other: The military seeks to maintain intact the boundaries the Kemalist state places on religion and to create structural barriers to prevent the AKP, or a party like it, from undermining the secular state or the military's role in it; the AKP wants to reduce the political influence of the military and to create more space for Islam in the public sphere.

After the AKP victory in the November 2002 elections, the chief of the Turkish General Staff (TGS), General Hilmi Özkök, sought to develop a *modus vivendi* with the AKP government. Özkök questioned the wisdom of military interventions in the past, expressed trust in the people's judgment, and did his best to insulate the military from day-to-day politics. The military departed from this accommodating position when confronted with what it perceived as attempts to undermine secularism. During the *İmam-Hatip* controversy, the military declared that the proposal to allow *İmam-Hatip* school graduates to compete on an equal footing with graduates of other educational institutions for admission to non-theology faculties of universities violated the secular premises of the republic.[52]

The military is particularly sensitive about issues relating to its internal cohesion. The Military High Council (YAS) regularly dismisses military personnel suspected of having Islamist tendencies. YAS decisions are not subject to appeal.[53] High-level AKP figures have frequently promised to amend the law to allow expelled officers to appeal in the courts, and Erdoğan has included a note expressing his reservations when signing the expulsion orders.[54] President Gül had done the same thing in the past.

The military, on the other hand, did not resist changes in civil-military relations that were introduced to bring Turkey's institutional framework more in line with EU standards. The most important of these changes was the reform of the National Security Council (*Milli Güvenlik Kurulu* (MGK)), which was divested of its executive power and turned into a purely advisory body; it went from a largely military membership to a civilian majority, with a civilian appointed as Secretary-General in 2004.[55]

Relations between the military and the AKP have become more strained since Özkök's replacement as chief of the TGS by General Yaşar Büyükanıt, former commander of the land forces, who is a

---

[52] Metin Heper, "The Justice and Development Party Government and the Military in Turkey," *Turkish Studies*, Vol. 6, No. 2, June 2005.

[53] In August 2007, the military dismissed 23 officers, 10 of them for fundamentalist activities.

[54] "Military Leaders, Erdoğan Meet to Discuss Promotions as Tensions Mount over Presidency," *Eurasia Daily Monitor*, The Jamestown Foundation, Vol. 4, Issue 149, August 1, 2007; for the TGS view, see "Chief of Staff Özkök: 'Reservations on YAS Decisions Have No Basis in the Law,'" *Turkish Press Review* 01.09.2003, at http://www.byegm.gov.tr/YAYINLA-RIMIZ/CHR/ING2003/01/03x01x09.HTM#%204 (as of March 21, 2008).

[55] The reform of the MGK was initiated by a secularist coalition government before the AKP took power. The reform was part of the seventh reform package, designed to harmonize Turkish legislation with the EU *acquis communitaire* and passed by parliament in July 2003.

strong secularist.[56] Islamist groups spearheaded a failed effort to block Büyükanıt's appointment. The campaign included allegations that Büyükanıt's grandfather was a Jew and that he was not a "true" Turk. A murky episode involving a request by a prosecutor in the southeastern town of Van to investigate Büyükanıt for attempting to influence the judiciary in the case of the November 2005 bombing of a bookshop in Şemdinli (for which two noncommissioned officers were indicted) threatened to escalate into a crisis. (The prosecutor said that General Büyükanıt had tried to influence a judicial process by praising one of the accused officers as a "good soldier.")[57] The military objected, claiming that the Van prosecutor "went beyond the limits of his authority," that the allegations had no legal basis, and that the list of charges was considered as an attack against the armed forces. General Özkök conveyed these objections first to Prime Minister Erdoğan and then to President Sezer.[58] In the end, a Ministry of Justice investigation found that the charges against Büyükanıt did not have "the required basis" for prosecution.[59]

Secularists and the military saw the campaign against Büyükanıt as part of a plan orchestrated by the AKP and Islamist sectors to undermine the military. (The CHP called it "a coup against the army.")[60] Their suspicions were strengthened by the fact that the prosecutor who

---

[56] Recently the media discovered that among all General Staff chiefs, only Özkök included the following phrase in his online CV: "Being accountable to the Prime Minister according to the Constitution . . ." The General Staff removed this phrase from the web site on July 7, 2007. "Özkök'ün tartışılan özgeçmişi değişti," *Hürriyet*, July 17, 2007.

[57] The Van Third Criminal Court's decision stated that the two noncommissioned officers found guilty of the crime could not have carried out the act without the involvement and protection of senior officers. *Turkish Daily News*, July 19, 2006, at http://www.turkishdailynews.com.tr/article.php?enewsid=49228 (as of March 21, 2008).

[58] "Allegations Against Land Forces Commander Cause Confusion in Ankara," TÜSİAD, *Turkey News*, March 1–7, 2006, at http://www.tusiad.us/specific_page.cfm?CONTENT_ID=588 (as of March 21, 2008).

[59] MEMRI, "The AKP and Other Turkish Islamists Attempt to Block Secular General from Top Military Post," Special Dispatch Series No. 1136, April 11, 2006, at http://memri.org/bin/articles.cgi?Page=archives&Area=sd&ID=SP113606 (as of March 21, 2008).

[60] "Allegations Against Land Forces Commander Cause Confusion in Ankara," op cit.

had requested the investigation of Büyükanıt, Ferhat Sarıkaya, was the same controversial prosecutor who had indicted the rector of Yüzüncü Yıl University in Van on corruption charges. (According to secularists, the rector was actually indicted because he had tried to prevent Islamist activities at the university.)[61] The AKP government's role in the Büyükanıt affair was ambiguous. The prime minister expedited the approval of Büyükanıt by parliament as a way of ending the controversy but did not (or could not) prevent his supporters from joining the anti-Büyükanıt campaign.

Tensions between the military and the AKP government mounted after Büyükanıt's selection as chief of the General Staff. In a speech at the end of September 2006 at the Istanbul Military Academy (while Erdoğan was on a visit to the United States), Büyükanıt called attention to the threat of Islamic fundamentalism, a warning echoed by other senior generals and by President Sezer. In an address at the Ankara Military Academy in early October 2006, Gen. Ilker Başbuğ, head of the land forces, told trainees that the "reactionary [Islamist] threat is reaching alarming proportions," accused Islamists of "patiently and systematically" eroding secularism, and defended the army's right to speak out on the issue despite EU criticism of military interference in politics.[62]

These tensions came to a head after the AKP decision to nominate Gül for the presidency. Gül's nomination provoked mass demonstrations by secularists in major Turkish cities; a warning by Büyükanıt in April; and the so-called e-coup or "midnight memorandum," a statement posted on the Turkish General Staff web site declaring that the military is "the definite defender of secularity" and "will manifest its attitude and behavior in an explicit and clear fashion when[63] necessary," which was perceived by many Turks as a veiled threat of a pos-

---

[61] Sarıkaya was later disbarred by the Supreme Board of Prosecutors and Judges (HSYK) for "dishonoring the legal profession" in a way deemed harmful to its public standing. *Turkish Daily News*, April 21, 2006.

[62] "Top Turkish General Warns of Islamist Threat," *Arab News*, September 26, 2006.

[63] Not "if."

sible military coup.[64] After the CHP and other parties boycotted the first round of voting in parliament, the Constitutional Court, which is dominated by secularists, supported the CHP's petition that the election was invalid because there had not been a quorum present.[65]

The failed presidential selection in May 2007 led to the decision to hold parliamentary elections, originally scheduled for November, on July 22, 2007. The AKP was embittered by the military's role in derailing Gül's candidacy for the presidency, although AKP critics contend that the party pushed the envelope too far by nominating him after Erdoğan decided not to stand for the presidency. In this view, the AKP abused its parliamentary majority—which represented only one-third of the electorate—to ram through the election of a candidate who was not broadly acceptable (i.e., to the secularist sector).

Gül's election as president on August 28, 2007, marks an important political watershed. For the first time in the history of the Turkish Republic, a non-secularist was elected president. This broke an important political tradition. However, it is unlikely to end the strains between the AKP and the military. The military harbors deep misgivings about Gül's election and has continued to manifest its discontent—as underscored by the military leadership's decision to boycott Gül's inaugural reception and swearing-in ceremony.[66] These pointed public displays of discontent are likely to continue. However, the AKP's overwhelming victory in the 2007 elections is likely to make the mili-

---

[64] Turkish General Staff Press Release, April 27, 2007.

[65] Some well-informed sources say that the TGS told Erdoğan that the military was opposed to his becoming president and that Erdoğan acquiesced. The compromise candidate was supposed to be Defense Minister Vecdi Gönül. However, according to these sources, Parliamentary Speaker Bülent Arınç (considered by secularists to be an unreconstructed Islamist and therefore even more objectionable than Erdoğan or Gül) objected and told Erdoğan that if Erdoğan was not the candidate, then it should be Gül or himself. Erdoğan chose Gül as the candidate likely to be the least objectionable to the military, but the military thought that it had an agreement with Erdoğan that a more broadly acceptable figure (i.e., someone whose wife did not wear a headscarf) would be the AKP candidate and felt betrayed when Gül's candidacy was announced. Discussions in Ankara and Istanbul, June 2007.

[66] "Icy winds blow between army and president," *Turkish Daily News,* August 30, 2007.

tary cautious about undertaking any direct intervention against the government unless it takes actions that clearly pose a threat to Turkey's secular order.

The AKP's Uncertain Future

The real threat confronting the AKP at the onset of Prime Minister Erdoğan's second term is not a direct intervention by the military, but rather a decision by the judiciary to close down the party. On March 14, 2008, the Public Prosecutor, Abdurrahman Yalçinkaya, forwarded a 162-page indictment to the Constitutional Court, requesting the closure of the AKP. The indictment accused the AKP and its leaders of violating the principles of secularism defined in Article 2 of the Turkish Constitution. It cited as evidence speeches and statements of President Gül, Prime Minister Erdoğan, and other AKP officials.[67]

The Constitutional Court is the highest legal authority in Turkey. It is composed of 11 members, who are appointed by the president, and is a bastion of secularism. The court accepted Yalçinkaya's indictment by a unanimous vote of 11–0.[68] The indictment has unleashed an internal crisis that potentially could have far-reaching consequences for Turkey's political future. If the court upholds the indictment, not only could the AKP be closed down, President Gül and Prime Minister Erdoğan, along with nearly 70 other AKP members, could be banned from politics for five years.

Closing down the AKP, however, is unlikely to eliminate it as a political force. As its strong showing in the Juy 2007 elections underscores, the AKP enjoys broad political support throughout the country. If it is closed, the party is likely to simply reemerge under another name—as happened when the MSP and the RP were banned. It

---

[67] For detailed analysis of the indictment and its possible political repercussions, see Hasan Kosebalaban, "The AKP Party Closure Case: Domestic Situation and International Reactions," Foundation for Political, Economic and Social Research (SETA), Policy Brief No. 10, April 2008, pp. 1–5.

[68] However, four members of the court objected to the inclusion of President Gül in the indictment. Under Turkish law, the president can be indicted only for treason.

would, however, sharpen the secularist-religious divide within Turkey and could lead some pious Turks to lose faith in the political system.

Turkey's prospects of EU membership, already facing serious obstacles, would be further jeopardized. Many EU members would use the ban as a reason to slow—or even suspend—accession negotiations. Even if, in the end, the AKP is not closed, the party will be preoccupied with its defense and its fight for political survival for many months. As a result, the impetus behind domestic reform, which has slowed since October 2005, is likely to languish, increasing strains in Turkey's relations with the EU.

CHAPTER FIVE

The AKP's Foreign Policy

The AKP's evolution has also been reflected in its foreign policy. In contrast to the National Salvation Party (MSP) and Welfare Party, which rejected ties to the West and pursued an anti-Western agenda, the AKP has maintained Turkey's Western orientation and has made strong ties to the West, particularly EU membership, an important pillar of its foreign policy. At the same time, the AKP has also sought to broaden and deepen Turkey's ties in other areas, particularly the Middle East, Central Asia and the Caucasus, and the Balkans.

This process of broadening and deepening Turkey's ties to areas beyond the West began well before the AKP came to power. Under Özal, for instance, Turkey made a concerted effort to establish closer ties to Central Asia. But efforts to expand Turkey's ties to areas where it has had strong historical and cultural ties have gained greater impetus under the AKP and have been heavily influenced by the doctrine of Strategic Depth, a concept developed by Ahmet Davutoğlu, a Turkish academic who became Erdoğan's chief foreign-policy advisor after the AKP won the November 2002 elections.[1] The core idea of the doctrine of Strategic Depth is that a nation's value in international relations

---

[1] See Ahmet Davutoğlu, *Stratejik Derinlik Türkiye 'nin Uluslararası Konumu*, Istanbul: Küre Yayınları, 2001. For a detailed discussion of the content and influence of the concept, see Alexander Murinson, "The Strategic Depth Doctrine in Turkish Foreign Policy," *Middle Eastern Studies*, Vol. 42, No. 6, November 2006, pp. 945–964. For an updated version that emphasizes the practical implementation of the doctrine, see Ahmet Davutoğlu, "Turkey's Foreign Policy Vision: An Assessment of 2007," *Insight Turkey*, Vol. 10, No. 1, 2008, pp. 77–96.

depends on its geostrategic location. Turkey is seen as particularly well suited to play an important geopolitical role because of its strategic location and control of the Bosporus.

In addition, the concept of Strategic Depth emphasizes the importance of Turkey's Ottoman past and its historical and cultural ties to the Balkans, the Middle East, and Central Asia. These ties are seen as important assets that can enable Turkey to become a regional power. The doctrine also suggests that Turkey should counterbalance its ties to the West by establishing multiple alliances, which would enhance its freedom of action and increase its leverage, both regionally and globally.

Davutoğlu's book was seen as little more than the musings of an academic with a pro-Islamic background when it was published in 2001. However, his elevation to the position of Erdoğan's chief foreign-policy advisor gave him the opportunity to directly influence Turkish foreign policy at the highest level. While it would be wrong to exaggerate Davutoğlu's influence in the formulation of Turkish foreign policy, many of his ideas, particularly his suggestion that Turkey should exploit its Ottoman legacy and play a more active role in the Middle East, have found strong resonance among AKP members and have been influential in shaping the broad contours of AKP policy.

The Strategic Depth concept is part of a larger debate in Turkey about the legacy of the Ottoman Empire, which has undergone a visible reassessment in recent years. While the Kemalists for decades denigrated the role of the Ottoman Empire and saw it as a hindrance to Turkey's modernization, many Turks have recently begun to view it in a more nuanced and positive light. Indeed, many, like Davutoğlu, see the Ottoman legacy as a positive building block that could enable Turkey to play a more active regional and global role.

Relations with Europe

The AKP has made close ties to Europe, especially EU membership, a central pillar of its foreign policy. At its summit in Brussels in December 2004, the EU agreed to open accession negotiations with Turkey, which formally began in October 2005. However, since then, relations with the EU have visibly cooled. Several factors have contributed to this cooling.

The first factor has been the slowdown of the internal reform process in Turkey. While the Erdoğan government initially gave internal reform a high priority, after the accession negotiations opened, the pace of reform slackened, aggravating relations with the EU. In addition, disenchantment with the EU has increased within parts of the AKP. The June 2004 decision by the European Court of Human Rights (ECHR) upholding the Turkish government's right to ban the headscarf came as a shock to many AKP members and led parts of the AKP to question whether an EU-oriented policy would really bring the benefits many had initially anticipated.

At the same time, popular support within Europe for further enlargement—and especially Turkish membership—has significantly declined since the French and Dutch referenda in May–June 2005. While the EU Commission supports continuing accession negotiations with Ankara, opposition to Turkish membership has increased, particularly in France and Germany, where a majority of the population opposes Turkish membership (see Figure 5.1).

Moreover, opposition to Turkish membership remains strong even if Turkey carries out reforms desired by EU members (see Figure 5.2). Much of the opposition appears to be based on religious and cultural grounds—a sense, noted earlier, that Turkey is not culturally a part of Europe. It also reflects growing popular concerns about the impact of large waves of Muslim immigrants on social stability.

The negative attitude in Europe toward Turkish membership has been matched by Turkey's growing disappointment with the EU. Public support in Turkey for EU membership, while still solid, has declined visibly over the past several years. Whereas in 2004, 73 percent of the Turkish population supported Turkish membership, that percentage dropped to 54 percent in 2006 and to 40 percent in 2007.[2] This decline

---

[2] *Transatlantic Trends: Key Findings 2007*, Washington, D.C: The German Marshall Fund of the United States, 2007, p. 22.

reflects a significant erosion of support and illustrates how the public mood in Turkey toward the EU has soured in the past several years.[3]

Despite these difficulties, the Erdoğan government remains committed to EU membership. In the wake of the July 22, 2007, elections Erdoğan promised to make a renewed effort to get relations with the EU back on track. However, reinvigorating the accession process may not be easy, for several reasons.

First, the election of Nicolas Sarkozy as French President has added a new obstacle to Turkey's membership ambitions. In contrast to former President Jacques Chirac, who supported Turkey's accession, Sarkozy is opposed to Turkish membership. Instead, he has proposed

Figure 5.1
European Public Opinion on Whether Turkey Should Be Invited to Join the EU

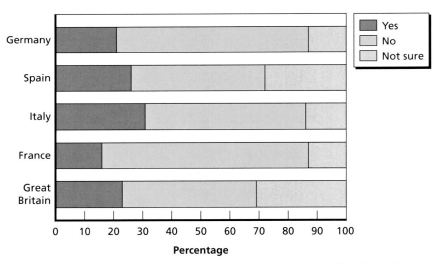

SOURCE: Harris Interactive, survey carried out May 31–June 12, 2007, with 6,169 respondents: Great Britain, 1,025; Germany, 1,014; France, 1,012; Italy, 1,090; Spain, 1,010; United States, 1,018, at http://www.harrisinteractive.com/news/allnewsbydate.asp?NewsID=1228 (as of March 21, 2008).
RAND MG726-5.1

---

[3] For a detailed discussion, see Mehmet Bardakçi, "Decoding the Rise of Euroskepticism in Turkey," *Insight Turkey*, Vol. 9, No. 4, 2007, pp. 116–123.

Figure 5.2
European Public Opinion: If Turkey Were to Implement Reforms Desired by Some EU Member States, Should It Be Invited to Join the EU?

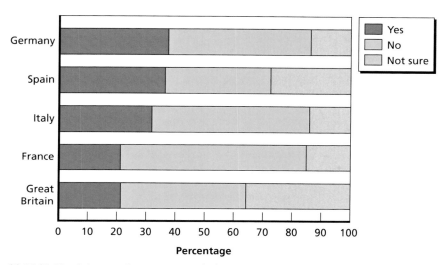

SOURCE: Harris Interactive, survey carried out May 31–June 12, 2007, with 4,526 respondents: Great Britain, 769; Germany, 839; France, 751; Italy, 726; Spain, 786; United States, 655, at http://www.harrisinteractive.com/news/allnewsbydate.asp? NewsID=1228 (as of March 21, 2008).
RAND MG726-5.2

giving Turkey a major role in a "Mediterranean Union" that would include France, Italy, Greece, Portugal, Spain, Malta, and Cyprus. However, this idea has little appeal in Ankara because it is seen as a substitute for EU membership.[4]

Erdoğan's domestic agenda may also collide with his EU agenda. His top priority is obtaining ratification of a new constitution to replace the 1982 constitution promulgated while Turkey was under military rule. This is likely to consume much of his time and energy in the early part of his second term. Other internal reforms advocated by the EU such as repeal of Article 301 of Turkey's penal code are likely to

---

[4] Fulya Özerkan, "EU talks about a bath in the Mediterranean," *Turkish Daily News*, May 30, 2007.

be postponed while he concentrates on getting the new constitution ratified.

The Kurdish issue, particularly the cross-border terrorist attacks conducted by the PKK from sanctuaries in northern Iraq, could also complicate Turkey's EU membership aspirations. While the increase in U.S. political and military support since Erdoğan's visit to Washington in early November 2007 should make it easier for him to manage the PKK problem, once the winter snows melt, the PKK is likely to renew its cross-border attacks against Turkey. The continued PKK threat could deflect the Erdoğan government's attention away from its domestic reform agenda, accentuating strains with the EU.

Civilian control of the military represents another obstacle. While the democratic reforms enacted in the past decade, especially those introduced by the Erdoğan government, have reduced the power of the military to intrude in politics, the EU has made it clear that stronger civilian control of the military is necessary if Turkey wants to become a member. However, the Turkish military views itself as the ultimate guarantor of secularism and has been reluctant to accept a further reduction of its political role at a time when it perceives growing internal and external threats to Turkey's security.

Finally, Cyprus remains a potential obstacle to Turkish membership. A Cyprus settlement is not part of the Copenhagen criteria governing membership, but many EU members are hesitant to admit Turkey as long as the issue remains unresolved. The Greek Cypriots overwhelmingly rejected the UN-brokered Annan Plan in May 2004, and negotiations remained suspended thereafter. However, the victory of Demetris Christofias, leader of the communist party (AKEL), in the Cypriot presidential elections in February 2008 has been welcomed by the Turkish Cypriot community and has revived hopes of possible new movement toward a settlement. A settlement of the Cyprus conflict would not only remove an important indirect obstacle to Turkey's membership in the EU, but could also give new impetus to improvements in Greek-Turkish relations. It would also eliminate an important impediment to closer cooperation between NATO and the EU.

Relations with Greece

Relations with Greece are one of the few bright spots on Turkey's European horizon. The Erdoğan government has continued the policy of détente that has been in place since 1999.[5] Indeed, Greek-Turkish relations are better today than they have been at any time since the Atatürk-Venizelos era in the 1930s. Trade has increased visibly, as have tourism and people-to-people exchanges. Energy cooperation has also intensified, bolstered by the opening of a $300 million gas pipeline that creates an energy corridor connecting the rich natural gas fields in the Caucasus with Europe.

This increased cooperation has given the Greek-Turkish relationship an important new dynamic and an element of stability. At the same time, it has served to decouple the Cyprus issue from Greek-Turkish bilateral relations. As a result, the danger of a Greek-Turkish conflict over Cyprus has significantly receded, and the Cyprus issue is less of an irritant in Greek-Turkish relations than it has been in the past.

Relations with the United States

Turkey's relations with the United States have experienced serious strains. Many of the current difficulties in U.S.-Turkish relations had their roots in the 1991 Gulf War. As Ian Lesser has noted, for many Turks the Gulf War is "the place where the trouble started."[6] The war created a de facto Kurdish entity under Western protection on Turkey's southern border, exacerbating Turkish concerns that an independent Kurdish state could one day emerge there.

---

[5] For background on the origins and initial impetus behind the rapprochement between Greece and Turkey since 1999, see F. Stephen Larrabee and Ian O. Lesser, *Turkish Foreign Policy in an Age of Uncertainty*, Santa Monica, CA: RAND Corporation, MR-1612-CMEPP, 2003, pp. 84–88.

[6] Ian Lesser, "Turkey, the United States, and the Geo-Politics of Delusion," *Survival*, Vol. 48, No. 3, Fall 2006, p. 2.

The U.S.-led invasion of Iraq intensified difficulties between Ankara and Washington. The Turkish leadership was strongly opposed to the invasion, fearing that it would result in an upsurge of instability on its southern border and aggravate its problem with the Kurds. In the aftermath of the invasion, the Turks have seen their worst fears realized. Iraq has been wracked by growing sectarian violence, while Iran's influence has increased, both regionally and in Iraq. Most important, from Turkey's perspective, the invasion has increased the possibility that an independent Kurdish state may eventually emerge on the Iraq-Turkey border, stimulating separatist pressures among Turkey's own Kurdish population.

These fears have been reinforced by the renewal of PKK terrorist attacks launched from sanctuaries in northern Iraq. Ankara has repeatedly requested U.S. assistance to help eliminate the PKK threat. Until recently, the United States has been reluctant to take military action against the PKK or to give the green light for the Turks to carry out a unilateral military strike against the PKK for fear that such actions could destabilize northern Iraq, which is relatively stable in comparison to the rest of the country, and could open a new front in the Iraq conflict.

The initial reluctance of the United States to take military action against the PKK sparked serious strains in relations with Turkey and contributed to a dramatic growth of anti-American sentiment in Turkey since 2004. Among Europeans, Turks have the lowest approval rating of President Bush's handling of international policies, with only 7 percent approving and 81 percent disapproving. The strongest negative feelings toward U.S. leadership are also found in Turkey, where 56 percent of respondents in 2006 viewed U.S. leadership as "undesirable."[7]

However, relations have begun to improve since Erdoğan's November 2007 visit to Washington. During the visit, President Bush agreed to provide Turkey with "actionable intelligence" against the PKK and appears to have given Erdoğan his backing for limited surgical strikes against the PKK camps in northern Iraq. Turkey has carried out a

---

[7] See *Transatlantic Trends: Key Findings 2006*, Washington, D.C.: German Marshall Fund of the United States, 2006, p. 19.

number of cross-border strikes against the PKK—reportedly with the aid of U.S. intelligence—but has avoided any major military incursion into northern Iraq on the scale of the incursions undertaken in the early 1990s.

Future relations will depend heavily on the nature of U.S. support for Turkey against the PKK. For Turkey, the PKK issue is the litmus test of the value of the U.S.-Turkish security partnership. If the United States continues to help Turkey eliminate, or at least significantly reduce, the PKK threat, U.S.-Turkish relations could gain positive new momentum. However, if U.S. cooperation against the PKK proves only temporary or begins to slacken, relations could deteriorate, contributing to greater instability in a region already rife with conflict.

In addition, differences have emerged over the issue of democracy promotion in the Middle East. While the Erdoğan government has been a strong advocate of greater transparency and democracy in the region, Turkish officials, especially the military, have been uncomfortable with U.S. attempts to portray Turkey as a "model" for Muslim countries in the Middle East. The military and the secular political establishment fear that the emphasis on the Middle East could weaken Turkey's Western identity and strengthen the role of Islam in Turkish society.[8]

Turkish officials insist that Turkey's path to democracy is not a model that can be implemented identically elsewhere in the Middle East. While they contend that Turkey's path can serve as an "inspiration" or point of reference for other Muslim societies, they emphasize that the Muslim countries in the Middle East have to "find their own

---

[8] In a toughly worded statement in April 2005 clearly aimed at the United States, Chief of the General Staff General Hilmi Özkök bluntly rejected the idea that Turkey could serve as a model for other Muslim countries, noting that "some circles try to define Turkey as a moderate Islamic country which could be an example for other Islamic countries. Turkey is not an Islamic country but a secular, democratic and social state that has adopted the rule of law." Özkök's remarks reflected the Turkish military's strong discomfort with U.S. efforts to depict Turkey as a model for other Muslim countries. See "Özkök talks tough," *Turkish Daily News*, April 21, 2005. Also "Özkök: Turkei kein modell," *Frankfurter Allgemeine Zeitung*, April 22, 2005.

solutions to their own problems" and that these solutions cannot be imposed from outside.[9]

The Armenian genocide issue has also been a source of discord between Ankara and Washington. Armenians and their supporters in the United States have sought periodically to introduce a resolution in Congress characterizing the tragedy that befell the Armenian people in 1915–1916 as a genocide—a characterization rejected by the Turks. In fall 2007, the Bush administration managed to prevent the resolution from coming to a vote, narrowly averting a potentially serious crisis with Ankara. However, the Armenian genocide issue is by no means dead. Proponents of the resolution, encouraged by its near success, are likely to intensify their efforts to secure its passage in the future. Thus the issue could reemerge as a potential source of discord in U.S.-Turkish relations.

Relations with Russia

During the Cold War, relations with Moscow were strained by Moscow's efforts to expand its power and influence in the Mediterranean and the Middle East, as well as its clandestine support for the PKK. However, since the end of the Cold War, Turkey's ties to Russia have visibly improved, especially in the economic realm. Russia is Turkey's second largest trading partner and its largest supplier of natural gas. An active suitcase trade has also emerged, which contributes significantly to the Turkish economy.

Energy has been an important driver of the closer ties between Turkey and Russia. Turkey imports 65 percent of its natural gas and 20 percent of its oil from Russia. If current trends continue, Turkish officials have suggested that the figure could increase to 80 percent in the coming years. Russian investment in Turkey, especially in the energy, tourism, and telecommunication sectors, has also grown visibly in recent years.

---

[9] See Abdullah Gül, "Turkey's Role in a Changing Middle East Environment," *Mediterranean Quarterly*, Vol. 15, No. 1, Winter 2004, pp. 2–7.

The improvement in ties to Moscow began well before the AKP came to power. However, it has accelerated under the Erdoğan government. In December 2004, President Putin became the first Russian head of state to visit Turkey in 32 years. The visit was crowned by a joint declaration on the "Deepening of Friendship and Multi-Dimensional Partnership," which makes reference to a wide range of common interests and the mutual trust and confidence that have developed between the two countries in recent years. Since then, high-level political and military contacts between Ankara and Moscow have intensified.

However, the emergence of a serious strategic alliance between Turkey and Russia in the near future seems highly unlikely. The two countries are rivals for influence in Central Asia and the Caucasus, where Russia has strong interests and neo-imperial ambitions. Moreover, a strategic alliance with Russia would require Turkey to curtail its ties to Europe, which accounts for more than 50 percent of its trade, and the United States, which despite recent differences, remains Turkey's most important ally and security partner.

Relations with the Middle East

Under the AKP, Turkish policy toward the Middle East has witnessed a new dynamism.[10] After decades of passivity and neglect, Turkey has begun to emerge as an important diplomatic actor in the region. Ankara has established close ties to Iran and Syria, two countries with which it had tense relations in the 1970s and 1980s. It has also adopted a more pro-Palestinian attitude in the Arab-Israeli conflict, and this has put pressure on its traditional ties with Israel.

This new activism in the Middle East represents an important departure in recent Turkish foreign policy, which, except for a brief period in the 1950s, has been characterized by caution and aloofness from deep involvement in Middle Eastern affairs. However, since the 1990–1991 Gulf War, Ankara has been increasingly drawn into Middle

---

[10] See F. Stephen Larrabee, "Turkey Rediscovers the Middle East," *Foreign Affairs*, Vol. 86, No. 4, July/August 2007, pp. 103–114.

East crises. For example, it was the host country to hundreds of thousands of Iraqi Kurdish refugees after the 1991 Gulf War and to U.S. operations to enforce the no-fly zone in northern Iraq.

Turkey's greater focus on the Middle East does not mean that it is turning its back on the West. Turkey remains strongly anchored in Western institutions, especially NATO. Nor does it reflect an "Islamization" of Turkish foreign policy, as some observers fear (although there are certainly elements within the AKP whose foreign-policy views are religiously motivated). Rather, it is primarily a response to structural changes in Turkey's security environment since the end of the Cold War. Today Turkey faces a much more diverse set of security threats and challenges, most of which are on its southern periphery. Thus Turkey has been forced to increase attention to the Middle East and become more deeply involved in Middle Eastern affairs.

Ankara's response to the Lebanon crisis in the summer and fall of 2006 provides an important example of Turkey's greater readiness to play a more active role in the Middle East. The Erdoğan government's decision to send 1,000 troops to participate in the UN peacekeeping force in Lebanon represented an important departure from Turkey's traditional policy of avoiding deep involvement in Middle Eastern affairs and provoked a heated internal debate. Such an action would have been unthinkable a few years ago. The decision provoked an open split between then President Sezer and Erdoğan. Sezer opposed Turkish participation in the UN peacekeeping force, arguing that it was "not Turkey's responsibility to protect others' national interests." Erdoğan, by contrast, maintained that Turkey could not afford to be a "mere bystander" and that the best way to protect Turkish national interests was to participate in the peacekeeping process.

The debate between Sezer and Erdoğan highlighted the difference between the traditional Turkish policy of avoiding deep involvement in Middle East crises and the more activist approach of Erdoğan and then Foreign Minister (now President) Abdullah Gül, who view engagement in the Middle East as essential to shaping developments on Turkey's periphery in directions conducive to Turkish interests.

Turkey's new activism in the Middle East is also reflected in Ankara's growing ties with Iran and Syria. In recent years, U.S. and Turkish policies toward Iran and Syria have increasingly diverged. The United States has sought to isolate both countries, whereas Turkey has intensified ties with them. While this rapprochement began prior to the election of the AKP, it has become more pronounced during the AKP's tenure in office and has exacerbated tensions with Washington.

The Kurdish issue has been an important driver in the intensification of Turkey's ties to both countries. Iran and Syria have substantial Kurdish minorities and share Turkey's interest in preventing the emergence of an independent Kurdish state. This shared interest has provided an important incentive for both countries to cooperate more closely with Ankara lately.

Energy has also been an important factor in Turkey's rapprochement with Iran, which is its second largest supplier of natural gas. While close cooperation with Iran over energy began in 1996 under the Erbakan government, it has intensified under Erdoğan. In July 2007, Turkey and Iran signed a Memorandum of Understanding (MOU) to transport 30 billion cubic meters of Iranian and Turkmen natural gas to Europe. The deal envisages the construction of two separate pipelines to ship natural gas from Iran and Turkmenistan to Europe. In addition, the state-owned Turkish Petroleum Corporation (TPAO) will be granted licenses to develop three different sections of Iran's South Pars gas field, which has estimated total recoverable reserves of 14 trillion cubic meters.[11]

The United States has strongly criticized the deal.[12] Washington opposes investment in Iran by third countries and favors transporting Turkmen gas by routes that avoid Iran. However, the Erdoğan government seems determined to go through with the deal. It argues that

---

[11] "Turkey Refuses to Back Down on Iran Energy Deal," *Eurasia Daily Monitor*, Vol. 4, No. 157, August 16, 2007.

[12] "US criticizes Turkey for Iran energy deal," *Turkish Daily News*, September 22–23, 2007; "US uneasy over Turkey Iran gas deal," *Turkish Daily News*, July 12, 2007; Ümit Eginsoy and Burak Ege Bekdil, "Turkish-Iranian Rapprochement Worries US," *Defense News*, August 6, 2007. See also "US critical of Turkey's partnership with Iran," *Turkish Daily News*, April 7, 2007.

Turkey needs to diversify its sources of supply in order to avoid becoming too dependent on one supplier. Moreover, the deal has strong domestic support and is part of the Erdoğan government's strategy to make Turkey a hub for the transport of Caspian energy to Europe.

Iran's nuclear ambitions, however, are a source of concern in Ankara. Turkey does not want to see the emergence of a nuclear Iran. Its concerns center not so much on fear of a direct attack by Iran as on the impact of Iran's acquisition of nuclear weapons on the regional military balance and the dangers of nuclear proliferation. Turkish officials fear that a nuclear-armed Iran could have a destabilizing impact on the Gulf region and could force Turkey to take countermeasures to safeguard its own security.

Turkey's relations with Syria have also improved significantly. As with Iran, the improvement began before the AKP came to power, but it has gained greater momentum since then. The rapprochement has been driven in particular by a common concern about the threat posed by Kurdish nationalism. Like Turkey, Syria faces an internal problem with its Kurdish minority, which has shown increasing signs of restlessness. The Ba'athist leadership around President Bashar Assad is concerned that the emergence of an economically robust Kurdish government in northern Iraq could stimulate pressures for economic and political improvements among Syria's Kurdish population and could pose a challenge to the regime's stability.

Turkey's relations with Israel have also undergone a shift under the AKP. The Erdoğan government has pursued a more active pro-Palestinian policy than its immediate predecessors did. Erdoğan has been openly critical of Israeli policy in the West Bank and Gaza, calling its actions "state terror."[13] Erdoğan also sharply criticized the Israeli invasion of Lebanon in response to Hezbollah's cross-border attack.

At the same time, the Erdoğan government has sought to establish closer ties to Hamas. A few weeks after the elections in the Palestinian territories, it hosted a delegation led by Khaled Mashaal, Hamas' Damascus-based hard-line political leader, in Ankara. The visit was

---

[13] "Israeli operation draws ire in Turkey," *The Probe,* May 23, 2004; "Turkey irked by Gaza offensive but not prompted to reverse ties to Israel," *The Probe,* May 30, 2004.

arranged without consultation with Washington and Jerusalem and greatly irritated both capitals because it directly undercut U.S. and Israeli efforts to isolate Hamas until it met a series of specific conditions, including acceptance of Israel's right to exist.[14]

The shift in policy toward Israel, however, has largely been one of tone and style. While Erdoğan has been more openly critical of Israeli policy than most previous Turkish leaders, this has not seriously affected the core of the relationship. Beneath the surface, cooperation in the defense and intelligence areas—which are handled by the Turkish military—has quietly continued and has been little influenced by the sharper public tone in Ankara's rhetoric.

Finally, Turkey has sought to improve ties to key Arab countries. Relations with Saudi Arabia have been strengthened, as highlighted by the visit of King Abdullah to Turkey in August 2006, the first visit of its kind in 40 years. Both countries have also tried to invigorate the Arab-Israeli peace process, as well as contain Iran's rising power. Ties to Egypt, another regional power, have also been strengthened. This enhanced cooperation between Turkey and Sunni Arab states in the Middle East reflects the growing recognition on the part of the Turkish leadership that stability on Turkey's southern border requires active engagement with its Middle Eastern neighbors and deeper participation in regional peace efforts.

However, there are important cultural and historical obstacles to a far-reaching intensification of Turkey's ties to the Muslim countries. As noted, Turkey's geopolitical interests are hardly aligned with Iran's nuclear ambitions and drive for regional hegemony. Moreover, Turks tend to look down on Arabs, while Arabs have not forgotten the centuries of imperial rule under the Ottomans and tend to be wary of

---

[14] The Hamas visit is often cited by critics as proof that the AKP's heart is in the Muslim world. The visit reflected differences within the Turkish government regarding how to react to the Hamas victory. The Turkish Foreign Ministry declined to extend an invitation to Mashaal. The invitation appears to have been extended by Erdoğan's chief foreign-policy advisor, Ahmet Davutoğlu. For a view arguing that the visit represents the AKP's true colors, see Soner Cagaptay, "Islamists in Charge," *The Wall Street Journal Europe*, August 18, 2006.

Turkish ambitions in the Middle East. Turkey's strong ties to Israel also pose an impediment to a far-reaching rapprochement with the Arab countries of the Middle East.

CHAPTER SIX

Future Prospects and Implications

In the past few years, the AKP has emerged as the dominant political force in Turkey. At the same time, it has undergone an important transformation, jettisoning the anti-Western rhetoric of the MSP and the Welfare Party and adopting a political agenda that emphasizes democracy, human rights, and Western integration. How deep-seated this transformation is and what impact it will have on Turkey's future political development and foreign-policy orientation, however, remain open questions. Turkey could evolve in a number of different ways over the next decade. In this chapter, we examine four possible alternative futures for Turkey and their implications for U.S. policy.

Whither Turkey: Alternative Political Futures

Scenario 1: The AKP Pursues a Moderate, EU-Oriented Path

In this scenario, the AKP solidifies its hold on power and maintains a moderate path, not allowing Islamist impulses in its domestic and foreign policy to derail its EU-oriented course. Some erosion of the restrictions on public expressions of religiosity occurs, and individuals are given greater latitude to express a more visible Islamic identity. However, no attempt is made to introduce Islamic legislation, such as Islamic legal codes. At the same time, efforts are made to reduce the political role of the military. An AKP government also seeks to loosen restrictions on religious minorities. There is a more open discussion of highly sensitive topics that Turkish society has found difficult to address, such as the Kurdish and Armenian questions.

In foreign policy, the AKP pursues an essentially EU-oriented course while simultaneously seeking to expand its ties to the Middle East. Opposition to Turkish membership remains strong in some key EU countries, but accession negotiations continue, providing international sanction for the AKP government's domestic political reform agenda. While still marred by occasional differences, Turkish-U.S. relations improve as the United States reduces its forces in Iraq and steps up cooperation against the PKK. Turkey continues to maintain close ties to Iran and Syria.

Until early 2008, this seemed to be the most likely scenario. However, the indictment of the AKP forwarded by the Public Prosecutor to the Constitutional Court in March 2008 has called this assumption into question. If, in the end, the AKP is not closed and remains in power, it is likely to be more cautious about pressing for measures that could be perceived as changing the secular-religious balance or provoking the secularists into anoter attempt to remove it from power.

The presence of AKP members and religious-school graduates in the government bureaucracy is likely to continue to expand, especially in the interior and education ministries, although it will do so much more slowly in Kemalist strongholds such as the foreign and defense ministries. At the local level, some AKP-run municipal councils are likely to continue efforts to infuse their conception of Islamic morality into public policy on issues such as restrictions on the sale of alcohol.

There are, however, structural limits on how far a reelected AKP government can go in opening space for Islam in the public sphere. The Kemalist establishment remains largely intact, and any government that crosses the lines that define the acceptable role of religion in politics risks accentuating political tensions and possibly provoking intervention by the military. Aside from the political constraints posed on the AKP's freedom of action by the military and secular elements in the bureaucracy, the judiciary, and the higher educational establishment, two other factors argue for a moderate course by an AKP government: One is the moderate and pluralistic tradition of Islam discussed in Chapter Two. Rigid Salafi interpretations of Islam have never taken root within a significant sector of the Turkish population, and public-opinion polls show that there is little support for an Islamic state. A large majority of Turks, including religious Turks, support the secular state.

The other factor arguing for a moderate course is that Turkey is imbedded in the West, institutionally, economically, strategically, and, to a significant degree, culturally. It is a member of NATO, the Council of Europe, the Organisation for Economic Co-operation and Development (OECD), and the Organization for Security and Co-operation in Europe (OSCE), and it is a candidate for EU membership. Over the past two decades, Turkey has converged significantly with European norms. Important gaps remain, but the trends are clear. The implication of this is that Islamic politics in Turkey are affected to a greater extent by the international context than is generally the case elsewhere. In this sense, the Turkish case is distinct from most of the rest of the Middle East.

A final consideration relates to the quality of AKP governance in its second term. Erdoğan's second government will be better able to steer a steady course if it is able to maintain economic stability and respond to security challenges in the southeast. The first AKP government was fortunate in that it did not face any major crises; therefore, its crisis-management skills have not been tested. However, an economic crisis (the current-accounts deficit has been alarmingly high for some time), a major lapse in the EU accession talks, or mishandling of the security situation on the country's southeastern border could significantly weaken the AKP government and reduce its freedom of action.

These considerations argue for a moderate trajectory for religious politics in a democratic and increasingly globalized Turkey. However, other, less positive outcomes are also possible in the Turkish case. Two possible alternatives are examined below.

Scenario 2: Creeping Islamization

In this scenario, the reelected AKP government pursues a more aggressive Islamist agenda. With full control of the executive and legislative branches of government, the AKP is able to appoint administrators, judges, and university rectors, and it can even influence personnel decisions in the military. In foreign policy, the AKP intensifies ties to the Muslim world, especially Iran and Syria. It adopts a much more openly pro-Palestinian position, while downgrading ties to Israel. Faced with growing opposition in Europe to its bid for EU membership, the AKP suspends accession negotiations and returns to an Erbakan-style effort to create a competing Islamic bloc.

"Creeping Islamization" is the scenario that worries most secularists, many of whom fear that the AKP harbors a hidden agenda to Islamize Turkish society and that its leadership may face pressure from the party's base to move more aggressively on social issues. However, in our view, this scenario is not very likely, for several reasons. First, it would lead to greater political polarization and would be apt to provoke intervention by the military. With the AKP in full control of the executive and legislative branches of government, the military can be expected to become more vigilant than ever regarding signs of creeping Islamization.

Second, as noted earlier, most Turks support a secular state and oppose a state based on the *shari'a*. Thus there would be little public support for an overt Islamist course. Third, achieving EU membership has been a core element of the AKP's foreign policy. Abandoning that goal would damage the AKP's prestige and credibility. While discontent with the EU has increased recently, EU membership is still supported by nearly half the Turkish population.

Scenario 3: Judicial Closing of the AKP

In this scenario, the Constitutional Court closes down the AKP. Closing down the AKP, however, would solve little and could lead to a deepening of the crisis. As its strong showing in the July 2007 elections underscores, the AKP enjoys broad political support throughout the country. If it is closed, the party is likely to simply reemerge under another name—as happened when the MSP and the RP were banned.

The closure of the AKP would be a setback to the Turkish experiment with the coexistence of an Islam-rooted party and secular democracy—a model that is being watched with interest in the Middle East. It could also increase Kurdish disaffection. The AKP enjoys strong support among Turkey's ethnic Kurdish population. Thus Turkey could face increasing unrest and growing separatist pressures among its Kurdish population. Finally, Turkey's prospects of EU membership, already facing serious obstacles, would be further jeopardized.

Scenario 4: Military Intervention

A fourth possibility is an escalation of social tensions that leads to intervention by the military. A confrontation could take place if the AKP takes actions seen by the military as crossing important lines. The intervention scenario has two possible variants: (1) a "soft coup," in which the military mobilizes social pressure against the AKP, eventually forcing it to resign, and (2) a direct military intervention leading to the forcible removal of the AKP government and the disbanding of the party.

A soft coup could be implemented through a decision by the Constitutional Court to dissolve the AKP and ban leading members from political activity on grounds of anti-secular activities. This was a modality employed against Erbakan's Virtue Party and may be the direction in which the secularist sector is moving. On March 31, 2008, the Constitutional Court voted unanimously to consider the case for the closure of the AKP brought by the public prosecutor for activities contrary to the principle of secularism.

While a direct intervention by the military cannot be excluded, especially if the AKP begins to push an Islamic agenda more aggressively, it is not very likely and would occur only as a last resort after the military had exhausted all other options. The military has been sobered by its previous direct interventions and has little enthusiasm for governing directly. In recent years, it has preferred to rely on indirect methods for achieving its goals.

Moreover, mobilizing society against the government, as the military did to force Erbakan's ouster in 1997, would be much harder with the AKP. The AKP was elected in a landslide victory with 47 percent of the vote. Unlike Erbakan's Welfare Party, which obtained only 21 percent of the vote, the AKP has broad-based popular support. Thus the military could not count on strong popular support for action against the AKP government.

The strong public reaction to the military's "midnight memorandum" of April 27, 2007, with its veiled threat of military intervention, underscores this point. The AKP's landslide victory represented a direct slap in the face for the military. Rather than rallying the population against the AKP, as it was intended to do, the memorandum actually increased support for it. This fact is unlikely to be lost on the military and may make it cautious about openly trying to mobilize opposition.

Implications for U.S. Policy

The rise of the AKP and the role of political Islam in Turkey have several broad implications for U.S. policy.

The first relates to the nature of political Islam in Turkey. Turkish Islam is more moderate and pluralistic than Islam elsewhere in the Middle East. Turkey has a long history of seeking to fuse Islam and Westernization, dating back to the late Ottoman period. This differentiates it from other Muslim countries in the Middle East and enhances the chances that it will be able to avoid the sharp dichotomies, ruptures, and violence that have characterized the process of political modernization in other Middle Eastern countries.

Second, the rise of political Islam in Turkey (or rather, of politics informed by Islam) has been largely a response to internal factors, particularly the democratization and socioeconomic transformation of Turkish society over the past several decades. External factors have played a secondary and far less consequential role. This, too, underscores Turkey's "exceptionalism" and differentiates Turkey from other Muslim countries in the Middle East.

This is important because it goes to the heart of the issue of the compatibility of Islam and democracy. The ability of a party with Islamic roots to operate within the framework of a secular democratic system while respecting the boundaries between religion and state would refute the argument that Islam cannot be reconciled with modern secular democracy. However, if the experiment fails, it could lead to greater polarization, further reducing the middle ground needed to build the moderate Muslim bulwark needed to contain the spread of radicalized Islam.

Nevertheless, policymakers should be cautious about portraying Turkey as a "model" for the Middle East. This notion makes many Turks, especially the secularists and the military, uncomfortable, because they feel it pushes Turkey politically closer to the Middle East and weakens its Western identity.[1] In addition, they fear that it will strengthen political Islam in Turkey and erode the principle of secularism over the long run. These concerns are particularly strong within the Turkish military.

Third, it is an oversimplification to see the current political tensions in Turkey as a struggle between "Islamists" and "secularists." Rather, these tensions are part of a struggle for power between newly emerging social sectors and the secularized elite—a struggle between the "periphery" and the "center" that has deep roots in Ottoman and recent Turkish history. The democratization of Turkish society since the mid-1980s has opened up political space for forces that had been largely excluded from politics (including Islamists) to organize and propagate their views.

Fourth, While the the AKP has Islamic roots, it enjoys broad-based political support that transcends religious, class, and regional differences. Its widespread social networks and efficient party machine, with close ties to local constituencies, have enabled it to gain strong support among the poor and the marginalized—many of whom are pious and socially conservative—who make up a growing portion of Turkey's urban population. At the same time, its liberal, free-market economic policies attract the provincial entrepreneurial classes in Anatolia—the so-called "Anatolian tigers"—which are socially conservative but integrated into the global economy.

The AKP's free-market economic policies also appeal to many secular businessmen in the larger cities who are attracted by the AKP's support for Turkish membership in the EU. Finally, the AKP's support for democratic reform and its tolerant policy toward minorities have enabled it to obtain the support of many Kurds, Alevis, and Armenians. In short, the AKP enjoys broad social support; it is not a narrow, religiously based party.

---

[1] See footnote 7 on p. 83.

Fifth, in the past decade, the AKP has undergone an important ideological transformation, abandoning the anti-Western rhetoric that characterized its predecessors, the National Salvation and Welfare parties, and embracing a new discourse that emphasizes values consistent with those of Western societies. This shift is most visible in the AKP's strong support for Turkey's efforts to achieve EU membership.

The shift has resulted in an important realignment in Turkish politics. In the past, the Kemalists were the main proponents of close ties to the West and Western integration. In recent years, however, this role has increasingly been assumed by the AKP as a result of its strong embrace of EU norms. Ironically, as the AKP has pressed forward with reforms designed to bring Turkey into conformity with EU norms and regulations, some sectors in the Kemalist establishment and the military have begun to worry that EU membership and further democratization could threaten Turkish security, as well as their own political role.

The indictment of the AKP presents the United States with a difficult dilemma. The United States has a strong stake in a stable, democratic Turkey and, beyond U.S. interests in Turkey, in the success of a political model that showcases the coexistence of a ruling Islam-rooted political party and secular democracy. An unstable Turkey wracked by internal dissension would make it even more difficult to stabilize Iraq and enhance regional stability in and around the Persian Gulf. The United States, therefore, should underscore its strong support for Turkish democracy. A U.S. approach would be more likely to be effective if it were made in coordination with the EU and European partners. However, in developing its position, the United States needs to tread lightly, lest perceived intervention in Turkey's internal affairs provoke a counterproductive nationalist reaction.

Turkey's prospects for attaining EU membership, however, remain uncertain. While the EU Commission supports continuing accession negotiations, opposition in Europe to Turkish membership is growing—on cultural as well as political grounds. At the same time, frustration and disenchantment with the EU are on the rise in Turkey. However, Erdoğan has invested too much to openly withdraw Turkey's membership application. Thus the accession negotiations are likely to continue—more out of inertia than of enthusiasm on Europe's part.

Although the United States is not a member of the EU, it has a stake in how the membership issue is managed. Turkey's integration into the EU will strengthen the EU and will give lie to the claim that the West—especially Europe—is innately hostile to Muslims. This could have a salutary effect on the West's relations with the Muslim world. Indeed, a moderate, democratic Turkey could act as an important bridge to the Middle East. However, rejection of Turkey's candidacy could provoke an anti-Western backlash, strengthening those forces in Turkey that want to weaken the country's ties to the West. Such a development is in the interest of neither the EU nor the United States.

Integrating a country of Turkey's size (nearly 70 million people), with large underdeveloped areas and very different cultural and religious traditions, presents a formidable challenge, especially at a time when the EU faces a daunting agenda of internal reform and restructuring. Given the sensitivity of the issue of Turkish membership within Europe, the United States should quietly support Turkish membership behind the scenes and avoid overt pressure. This could anger EU members and even hurt Turkey's membership chances.

At the same time, Washington needs to recognize that Turkish membership in the EU would have an impact on the tone and character of U.S.-Turkish relations over the long run. While Ankara would continue to want strong security ties to the United States, Turkish leaders would look increasingly to Brussels rather than Washington on many issues. As a result, Turkey's foreign policy would be likely to become more "Europeanized" over time.

Foreign Policy and Bilateral Issues

The Middle East is likely to remain a sensitive issue in bilateral U.S.-Turkish relations. Turkey's growing interests in the Middle East are likely to make Ankara wary about allowing the United States to use its military facilities for Middle East and Persian Gulf contingencies except where such operations are clearly perceived to be in Turkey's interest. The United States therefore cannot automatically count on being able to use Turkish bases in Middle East operations. This argues for a diversification of U.S. access options in the Middle East that would provide alternatives to Incirlik Air Base should Turkey increase restrictions on U.S. use of it or other Turkish facilities.

The Armenian genocide resolution periodically introduced in the U.S. Congress could also cause strains in relations with Ankara. In 2007, the Bush administration succeeded in getting the genocide resolution (HR-106) shelved at the last second, narrowly averting a serious crisis with Ankara. However, the resolution is likely to be reintroduced in the future and remains a potential source of discord. If the resolution were to pass, the Turkish government could come under domestic pressure to take retaliatory action, possibly curtailing U.S. access to İncirlik and other Turkish facilities.

The question of the responsibility for the deaths of untold numbers of Armenians in 1915–1916 is an important moral and political issue. But it is one best left to historians. Passage of a genocide resolution will do nothing to foster closer Turkish-Armenian reconciliation. On the contrary, it will stimulate a nationalist backlash in Turkey and will make reconciliation more difficult, at the same time causing great potential damage to U.S.-Turkish relations at a moment when closer cooperation is vital to help stabilize Iraq and the broader Middle East. Thus, the executive branch will need to work closely with the congressional leadership to keep the issue from poisoning relations with Ankara.

The PKK and the Kurdish Issue

The United States also needs to deal more resolutely with the PKK terrorist attacks against Turkish territory. For Turkey, the PKK issue is the litmus test of the value of the U.S.-Turkish security partnership. The U.S. reluctance to help Turkey address this issue more forthrightly has been the primary cause of current strains in relations with Ankara and the dramatic rise in anti-American sentiment in Turkey since 2004.

Closer military and intelligence cooperation with Ankara against the PKK since Erdoğan's visit to Washington in November 2007 has helped to defuse some of the mistrust and tension in bilateral relations that have built up since—and to a large degree as a consequence of—the invasion of Iraq. But it needs to be followed up by other concrete steps. In particular, the United States needs to put greater pressure on the Kurdistan Regional Government (KRG) to crack down on the PKK and cease its logistical and political support of the group.

However, the PKK threat cannot be resolved by military means. While a tough anti-terrorist program is an important component of a long-term strategy to defeat the PKK, it must be combined with social and economic reforms that address the root causes of the Kurdish grievances.

In addition, the United States should encourage Turkey to enter into a direct dialogue with the KRG leadership in northern Iraq. There can be no stability on Turkey's southern border over the long term without an accommodation with the KRG. This does not mean that Turkey should recognize an independent Kurdish state, but it does need to find a stable *modus vivendi* with the KRG, whose cooperation is essential to reduce the PKK threat.

Bibliography

Books

Arjomand, Said (ed.), *From Nationalism to Revolutionary Islam,* London: Macmillan, 1984.

Bardakoğlu, Ali, *Religion and Society: New Perspectives from Turkey,* Ankara: Presidency of Religious Affairs, 2006.

Birand, Mehmet Ali, *The Generals' Coup in Turkey,* London: Brassey's Defense Publishers, 1987.

Çarkoğlu, Ali, and Binnaz Toprak, *Değişen Türkiye'de Din, Toplum ve Siyaset,* Istanbul: TESEV, 2006.

———, *Türkiye'de Din, Toplum ve Siyaset,* Istanbul: TESEV, 2000.

Davutoğlu, Ahmet, *Stratejik Derinlik Turkiye 'nin Uluslararasi Konumu,* Istanbul: Kure Yayinlari, 2001.

Ergil, Doğu, *Secularism in Turkey: Past and Present*, Ankara: Turkish Foreign Policy Institute, 1995.

Heper, Metin, and Ahmet Evin, *State, Democracy and the Military: Turkey in the 1980s,* Berlin/New York: Walter de Gruyter, 1988.

Kinross, Lord, *The Ottoman Centuries: The Rise and Fall of the Turkish Empire*, New York: Morrow Quill, 1977.

———, *Ataturk,* New York: William Morrow, 1964.

Kinzer, Stephen, *Crescent and Star: Turkey Between Two Worlds*, New York: Farrar, Straus and Giroux, 2001.

Larrabee, F. Stephen, and Ian O. Lesser, *Turkish Foreign Policy in an Age of Uncertainty*, Santa Monica, CA: RAND Corporation, MR-1612-CMEPP, 2003.

Lesser, Ian O., *Beyond Suspicion: Rethinking US-Turkish Relations*, Washington, D.C.: Woodrow Wilson Center, 2007.

Lewis, Bernard, *The Emergence of Modern Turkey,* 2nd ed., London: Oxford University Press, 1968.

Mango, Andrew, *Ataturk*, New York: The Overlook Press, 1999.

Özcan, Hüseyin, *Alevi-Bektaşi: Kültürüne Bakışlar*, Istanbul: Horasan Yayınları, 2003.

Rabasa, Angel, Cheryl Benard, Peter Chalk, C. Christine Fair, Theodore W. Karasik, Rollie Lal, Ian O. Lesser, and David E. Thaler, *The Muslim World After 9/11*, Santa Monica, CA: RAND Corporation, MG-246-AF, 2004.

Roy, Oliver, *Globalized Islam: The Search for a New Ummah*, New York: Columbia University Press, 2006.

Rubin, Barry, *Political Parties in Turkey*, London: Frank Cass and Company Ltd., 2002.

Rubin, Barry, and Kemal Kirişci (eds.), *Turkey in World Politics: An Emerging Multiregional Power,* Boulder, CO: Lynne Rienner Publishers, 2001.

Toprak, Binnaz, *Islam and Political Development in Turkey*, Leiden, The Netherlands: E. J. Brill, 1981.

Ünal, Ali, and Alphonse Williams (eds.), *Advocate of Dialogue: Fethullah Gülen,* Fairfax, VA: The Fountain, 2000.

White, Jenny B., *Islamic Mobilization in Turkey: A Study in Vernacular Politics,* Seattle and London: University of Washington Press, 2002.

Yavuz, M. Hakan, and John L. Esposito, *Turkish Islam and the Secular State: The Gülen Movement*, Syracuse, NY: Syracuse University Press, 2003.

Monographs, Articles, and Papers

AK Parti Program, August 14, 2001. As of February 28, 2008: http://eng.akparti.org.tr/english/partyprogramme.html

Akkoç, Serkan, "Almanya'da Kanal 7 ve Deniz Feneri'ne kara para baskını," *Hürriyet*, April 26, 2007.

Aksit, Bahattin, cited in Henry Rutz, "The Rise and Demise of İmam-hatip Schools: Discourses of Islamic Belonging and Denial in the Construction of Turkish Civil Culture," *PoLAR: Political and Legal Anthropology Review*, Vol. 22, No. 2, November 1999. As of February 29, 2008: http://www.anthrosource.net/doi/abs/10.1525/pol.1999.22.2.93

Akyol, Mustafa, "Meet Turkey's Real Islamists," *Turkish Daily News*, July 19, 2007. As of March 1, 2008: http://www.turkishdailynews.com.tr/article.php?enewsid=78690

"Alevis await decision on house of worship status for Cem evleri," *Today's Zaman*, June 22, 2007. As of February 28, 2008:
http://www.todayszaman.com/tz-web/detaylar.do?load=detay&link=114687

"Alevis vote based on individual decisions," *Today's Zaman*, July 18, 2007.

"Allegations Against Land Forces Commander Cause Confusion in Ankara," TÜSİAD, *Turkey News*, March 1–7, 2006. As of March 1, 2008:
http://www.tusiad.us/specific_page.cfm?CONTENT_ID=588

Allen, John L., Jr., "These two Islamic movements bear watching," *All Things Catholic*, National Catholi Reporter, June 22, 2007. As of March 1, 2008:
http://ncrcafe.org/node/1188

"Alman polisinden Kanal 7 INT'e baskın," *Radikal,* April 26, 2007.

Armutçu, Oya, "61 yaşında emekliliğe iptal," *Hürriyet*, October 9, 2003.

Atacan, Fulya, "Explaining Religious Politics at the Crossroad: AKP-SP," *Turkish Studies*, Vol. 6, No. 2, June 2005, pp. 187–199.

Atalar, M. Kürşad, "Hizballah of Turkey: A Pseudo-Threat to the Secular Order?" *Turkish Studies,* Vol. 7, No. 2, July 2006.

Aydin, Mustafa, "Moving Beyond Iraq: Reconstruction," *Private View,* Istanbul, No. 12, Autumn 2007.

Ayman, Gülden, "Turkish-American Relations and the Future of Iraq," *Private View,* Istanbul, No. 12, Autumn 2007.

Bacık, Gökhan, "An Emerging Friendship: Turkey and Syria," *Insight Turkey,* Vol. 9, No. 3, 2007.

Bardakçi, Mehmet, "Decoding the Rise of Euroskepticism in Turkey," *Insight Turkey*, Vol. 9, No. 4, 2007.

Barkey, Henri J., "The Struggles of a 'Strong' State," *Journal of International Affairs*, Vol. 54, No. 2, Fall 2000.

Başkan, Filiz, "The Fethullah Güllen Community: Contribution or Barrier to the Consolidation of Democracy in Turkey?" *Middle Eastern Studies,* Vol. 41, No. 6, November 2005.

"Beş İslami derneğin yükselişi," *Radikal,* April 27, 2007.

"Biography of Prof. Dr. Mahmud Esad Cosan," undated. As of February 28, 2008:
http://gumushkhanawidargah.8m.com/friday/mec.html

Birch, Andrew, "Turkey: The Search for a New Central Bank Governor," *Global Insight*, March 29, 2006. As of February 28, 2008:
http://www.globalinsight.com/Perspective/PerspectiveDetail2936.htm

"Biz Kimiz," Deniz Feneri Derneği, January 30, 2003. As of February 28, 2008:
http://www.denizfeneri.org.tr/icerik.asp?kategori=KURUMSAL.

Boland, Vincent, "Military's strategy to neutralize opponents is big casualty of poll," *Financial Times*, July 24, 2007.

Bölme, Selin, "The Politics of Incirlik Air Base," *Insight Turkey*, Vol. 9, No. 3, 2007.

"A bomb-builder, 'out of the shadows,'" *The Washington Post*, February 20, 2006.

Bonfil, Metin, "From Challenge to Opportunity, to Challenge Again," *Private View*, Istanbul, No. 12, Autumn 2007.

Bonner, Arthur, "An Islamic Reformation in Turkey," *Middle East Policy*, Vol. XI, No. 1, Spring 2004.

"Büyükanıt Warns AKP on Constitution, DTP on PKK," *Eurasia Daily Monitor*, The Jamestown Foundation, Vol. 4, Issue 182, October 2, 2007.

Cagaptay, Soner, "Can the PKK Renounce Violence? Terrorism Resurgent," *Middle East Quarterly*, Winter 2007. As of February 28, 2008:
http://www.meforum.org/article/1060.

————, "Islamists in Charge," *The Wall Street Journal Europe*, August 18, 2006.

————, "Turkish Troubles," *The Wall Street Journal Europe*, July 30, 2007. As of March 2, 2008:
http://online.wsj.com/public/article/SB118574382583581533.html.

————, "How Will the Turkish Military React?" Madrid: Real Instituto Elcano, July 16, 2007.

————, "Secularism and Foreign Policy in Turkey," The Washington Institute for Near East Policy, Policy Focus #67, April 2007.

————, "Symposium: Turkey: The Road to Sharia?" FrontPageMagazine.com, May 6, 2005. As of March 2, 2008:
http://www.danielpipes.org/article/2592

————, "Turkey at a Crossroads: Preserving Ankara's Western Orientation," The Washington Institute for Near East Policy, Policy Focus #48, 2005.

Çandar, Cengiz, "Democracy has won a victory," *Turkish Daily News*, July 24, 2007.

Çetinsaya, Gökhan, "Turkey and the New Iraq," *Insight Turkey*, Vol. 8, No. 2, April–June 2006.

————, "Rethinking Nationalism and Islam: Some Preliminary Notes on the Roots of 'Turkish-Islamic Synthesis' in Modern Turkish Political Thought," *The Muslim World*, Vol. 89, Issue 3-4, October 1999, pp. 350–376. As of February 28, 2008:
http://www.blackwell-synergy.com/doi/abs/10.1111/j.1478-1913.1999.tb02753.x

"Chief of Staff Ozkok: 'Reservations on YAS Decisions Have No Basis in the Law," *Turkish Press Review* 01.09.2003. As of March 1, 2008: http://www.byegm.gov.tr/YAYINLARIMIZ/CHR/ING2003/01/03x01x09. HTM#%204

"Court says senior officers involved in Şemdinli bombing," *Turkish Daily News*, July 19, 2006. As of March 1, 2008: http://www.turkishdailynews.com.tr/article.php?enewsid=49228

Dağı, İhsan, "Turkish Politics at the Crossroads," presentation at the German Marshall Fund of the United States conference, Washington, D.C., February 8, 2007.

———, "Transformation of Islamic Political Identity in Turkey: Rethinking the West and Westernization," *Turkish Studies*, Vol. 6, No. 1, March 2005, pp. 21–37.

Davutoğlu, Ahmet, "Turkey's Foreign Policy Vision: An Assessment of 2007," *Insight Turkey*, Vol. 10, No. 1, 2008.

Demiralp, Seda, and Todd A. Eisenstadt, *Prisoner Erdogan's Dilemma and the Origins of Moderate Islam in Turkey*, Washington, D.C.: American University, Department of Government, August 31, 2006.

Demirkan, Süleyman, "Çiğdem Toker, 61 yaşında emeklilik telaşı," *Hürriyet*, March 18, 2003.

"Deniz Feneri'nin kuryeleri belirlendi," *Hürriyet,* June 18, 2007.

Deutsche Botschaft Ankara, undated. As of February 28, 2008: http://www.ankara.diplo.de/Vertretung/ankara/tr/01/stag.html

Eğilmez, Mahfi, "The World and Turkey Cannot Go in Separate Directions," *Private View,* Istanbul, No. 12, Autumn 2007.

Eginsoy, Umit, and Burak Ege Bekdil, "Turkish-Iranian Rapprochement Worries US," *Defense News*, August 6, 2007.

Eligür, Banu, "Are Former Enemies Becoming Allies? Turkey's Changing Relations with Syria, Iran, and Israel Since the 2003 Iraqi War," Waltham, MA: Brandeis University, Crown Center for Middle East Studies, Middle East Brief No. 9, August 2006.

———, "Turkish-American Relations Since the 2003 Iraqi War: A Troubled Partnership," Waltham, MA: Brandeis University, Crown Center for Middle East Studies, Middle East Brief No. 6, May 2006.

Erdem, Zihni, and Ahmet Kıvanç, "Gurbetçi parası RP ve FP'ye," *Radikal*, December 16, 2005.

Erdermir, Aykan, "Tradition and Modernity: Alevis' Ambiguous Terms and Turkey's Ambivalent Subjects," *Middle Eastern Studies,* Vol. 41, No. 6, November 2005.

Erel, İsmail, "Kanal 7 müdürü tutuklandı 8 milyon Euro aranıyor," *Hürriyet,* April 27, 2007.

Ergil, Doğu, "Identity Crises and Political Instability in Turkey," *Journal of International Affairs*, Vol. 54, No. 2, Fall 2000.

Erman, Tahire, and Emrah Göker, "Alevi Politics in Contemporary Turkey," *Middle Eastern Studies,* Vol. 36, No. 4, October 2000.

"An Evaluation Related to the Net Error and Omission Item in the Balance of Payments," November 2005. As of February 28, 2008: http://www.tcmb.gov.tr/yeni/evds/yayin/kitaplar/Net%20Hata%20ve%20Noksan.pdf

Faltas, Sami, and Sander Jansen (eds.), *Governance and the Military: Perspectives for Change in Turkey,* Groningen, The Netherlands: Centre for European Security Studies, May 2006.

Göle, Nilüfer, "Secularism and Islamism in Turkey: The Making of Elites and Counter-Elites," *Middle East Journal,* Vol. 51, No. 1, Winter 1997.

Göner, Özlem, "The Transformation of the Alevi Collective Identity," *Cultural Dynamics*, Vol. 17, No. 2, 2005. As of February 28, 2008: http://cdy.sagepub.com/cgi/content/abstract/17/2/107

Gül, Abdullah, "Turkey's Role in a Changing Middle East Environment," *Mediterranean Quarterly*, Vol. 15, No. 1, Winter 2004, pp. 2–7.

Gülalp, Haldun, "Globalization and Political Islam: The Social Bases of Turkey's Welfare State," *International Journal of Middle East Studies,* Vol. 33, No. 3, August 2001.

———, "Political Islam in Turkey: The Rise and Fall of the Refah Party," *The Muslim World,* Vol. 89, No. 1, January 1999.

Gunay, Niyazi, "Implementing the 'February 28' Recommendations: A Scorecard," *Research Notes No. 10*, Washington, D.C.: Washington Institute for Near East Policy, May 2001.

Harris Interactive, FT/Harris Poll, 2007. As of March 1, 2008: http://www.harrisinteractive.com/news/allnewsbydate.asp?NewsID=1228

Heper, Metin, "The Justice and Development Party Government and the Military in Turkey," *Turkish Studies*, Vol. 6, No. 2, June 2005.

———, "The Ottoman Legacy and Turkish Politics," *Journal of International Affairs*, Vol. 54, No. 1, Fall 2000.

———, "The Problem of the Strong State for the Consolidation of Democracy," *Comparative Political Studies*, Vol. 25, July 1992.

"Hepimiz Ermeniyiz," *Hürriyet*, January 20, 2007.

"Icy winds blow between army and president," *Turkish Daily News,* August 30, 2007.

İlk Parlamento, Geçmişten Günümüze TBMM, Türkiye Büyük Millet Meclisi. As of February 27, 2008:
http://www.tbmm.gov.tr/tarihce/kb2.htm

"İnsani yardım kuruluşları tek çatı altında birleşecek," *Hürriyet,* February 24, 2007.

"Is a New Wave of Terrorism Starting Against Turkey?" *Pulse of Turkey,* No. 68, November 7, 1998. As of February 28, 2008:
http://www.turkpulse.com/is.htm

"Israeli operation draws ire in Turkey," *The Probe,* May 23, 2004.

KADIP (Kültürlerarasi Diyalog Platformu), Intercultural Dialogue Platform, Istanbul, 2007.

Kahraman, Hasan Bülent, "Turkey Since 2002 and Beyond 2007," *Private View,* Istanbul, No. 12, Autumn 2007.

Kaleağasi, Bahadır, "Turkey Watch/EU: Common European Values and Interests Are the Basis of Turkey's EU Membership Process," *Private View,* Istanbul, No. 12, Autumn 2007.

Kanlı, Yusuf, "Confidence crisis between Erdoğan and EU," *Turkish Daily News,* September 20, 2004.

Karakas, Cemal, *Turkey: Islam and Laïcism Between the Interests of the State, Politics and Society,* Peace Research Institute Frankfurt (PRIF), Report No. 78, 2007.

Kaya, Ayhan, "Euro Turks: Dwelling in a Space of Their Own," *Private View,* Istanbul, No. 12, Autumn 2007.

Keskin, Adnan, "Endüstri' davası emsal oluyor, yeşil şirketlere 'çete' kıskacı," *Radikal,* January 31, 2007.

"Kombassan ve Yimpaş'ta şok," *Radikal,* June 16, 2007.

"Komisyon önerdi: Hükümet dinlemedi," *Radikal,* November 1, 2006.

Kosebalaban, Hanan, "The AKP Party Closure Case: Domestic Situation and International Reactions," Foundation for Political, Economic and Social Research (SETA), Policy Brief No. 10, April 2008.

Landau, Jacob, "The National Salvation Party in Turkey," *Asian and African Studies*, Vol. 11, 1976, pp. 1–57.

Landler, Mark, and Nicholas Kulish, "Turkish connection shakes Germans," *International Herald Tribune*, September 8–9, 2007.

Larrabee, F. Stephen, "Turkey Rediscovers the Middle East," *Foreign Affairs*, Vol. 86, No. 4, July/August 2007, pp. 103–114.

Lesser, Ian O., "Rethinking US-Turkish Relations," *Insight Turkey,* Vol. 9, No. 3, 2007.

———, "Turkey, the United States, and the Geo-Politics of Delusion," *Survival,* Vol. 48, No. 3, Fall 2006.

———, "Turkey: 'Recessed' Islamic Politics and Convergence with the West," in Rabasa et al., *The Muslim World After 9/11*, Santa Monica, CA: RAND Corporation, MR-246-AF, 2004, pp. 175–205.

Marcus, Aliza, "Turkey's PKK: Rise, Fall, Rise Again?" *World Policy Journal*, New York: NYU Press, Spring 2007.

Mardin, Şerif, "Turkish Islamic Exceptionalism Yesterday and Today," *Journal of International Affairs,* Vol. 54, No. 1, Fall 2000.

———, "Center-Periphery Relations. A Key to Turkish Politics?" *Daedalus*, Vol. 102, No. 1, Winter 1973, pp. 169–190.

———, "Ideology and Religion in the Turkish Revolution," *International Journal of Middle East Studies,* Vol. 2, No. 3, July 1971.

MEMRI, "The AKP and Other Turkish Islamists Attempt to Block Secular General from Top Military Post," Special Dispatch Series No. 1136, April 11, 2006. As of March 1, 2008:
http://memri.org/bin/articles.cgi?Page=archives&Area=sd&ID=SP113606

Michel, Thomas, S.J., "Muslim-Christian Dialogue and Cooperation in the Thought of Bediuzzaman Said Nursi," *The Muslim World,* Vol. 88, No. 3-4, July–October 1999. As of March 2, 2008:
http://www.blackwell-synergy.com/doi/pdf/10.1111/j.1478-1913.1999.tb02751.x

"Military Leaders, Erdoğan Meet to Discuss Promotions as Tensions Mount over Presidency," *Eurasia Daily Monitor*, The Jamestown Foundation, Vol. 4, Issue 149, August 1, 2007.

Murinson, Alexander, "The Strategic Depth Doctrine in Turkish Foreign Policy," *Middle Eastern Studies*, Vol. 42, No. 6, November 2006, pp. 945–964.

Narlı, Nilüfer, "The Rise of the Islamist Movement in Turkey," *Middle East Review of International Affairs,* Vol. 3, No. 3, September 1999.

"New Draft Turkish Constitution Foresees Easing Restrictions on Religious and Ethnic Identity," *Eurasia Daily Monitor*, The Jamestown Foundation, Vol. 4, Issue 169, September 13, 2007.

Novak, Robert, "Bush's Turkish Gamble," *Washington Post*, July 30, 2007.

Öniş, Ziya, "The Political Economy of Islamic Resurgence in Turkey: The Rise of the Welfare Party in Perspective," *Third World Quarterly,* Vol. 18, No. 4, September 1997.

Özbudun, Ergun, "Why the Crisis over the Presidency?" *Private View,* Istanbul, No. 12, Autumn 2007.

Özel, Soli, "Turkey Faces West," *Wilson Quarterly,* Vol. 31, No. 1, Winter 2007.

Özerkan, Fulya, "EU talks about a bath in the Mediterranean," *Turkish Daily News,* May 30, 2007.

Özgür, Bahadır, "The Naqshi Kurdish Opposition Hit the DTP Where It Hurts," *Turkish Daily News,* August 6, 2007. As of March 1, 2008: http://www.turkishdailynews.com.tr/article.php?enewsid=80163

"Ozkok talks tough," *Turkish Daily News,* April 21, 2005.

"Ozkok: Turkei kein modell," *Frankfurter Allgemeine Zeitung,* April 22, 2005.

"Özkök'ün tartışılan özgeçmişi değişti," *Hürriyet,* July 17, 2007.

Peuch, Jean-Christophe, "Turkey: What Remains of Political Islam?" Radio Free Europe/Radio Liberty. As of March 21, 2008: www.Rferl.org/features/2003/01/10012003163109.asp

"Poorer, Less Educated Voters Prefer Turkey's AK Party," *Eurasia Daily Monitor,* The Jamestown Foundation, Vol. 4, Issue 148, July 31, 2007.

Posch, Walter, "Crisis in Turkey: Just Another Bump on the Road to Europe?" Paris: The European Institute for Security Studies, Occasional Paper No. 67, June 2007.

"Progress Report on Turkey's EU Accession Process" (Turkish), 2002. As of February 28, 2008: http://www.abgs.gov.tr/files/AB_Iliskileri/AdaylikSureci/IlerlemeRaporlari/Turkiye_Ilerleme_Rap_2002.pdf

Rubin, Michael, "Will Turkey Have an Islamist President?" *Middle Eastern Outlook,* American Enterprise Institute for Foreign Policy Research, No. 1, February 2007.

Rutz, Henry, "The Rise and Demise of Imam-Hatip Schools: Discourses of Islamic Belonging and Denial in the Construction of Turkish Civil Culture," *PoLAR: Political and Legal Anthropology Review,* November 1999, Vol. 22, No. 2. As of March 2, 2008: http://www.anthrosource.net/doi/abs/10.1525/pol.1999.22.2.93

Sandberk, Özdem, "Testing Times They Are..." *Private View,* Istanbul, No. 12, Autumn 2007.

Schiffauer, Werner, "Islamism in the Diaspora: The Fascination of Political Islam Among Second Generation German Turks," unpublished paper, Frankfurt/Oder: Europea-Universität Viadrina, 1999.

Tank, Pınar, "Political Islam in Turkey: A State of Controlled Secularity," *Turkish Studies,* Vol. 6, No. 1, March 2005.

Toktaş, Şule, "Perceptions of Anti-Semitism Among Turkish Jews," *Turkish Studies*, Vol. 7, No. 2, June 2006.

"Top Turkish General Warns of Islamist Threat," *Arab News*, September 26, 2006.

Toprak, Binnaz, "Islam and Democracy in Turkey," *Turkish Studies*, Vol. 6, No. 2, June 2005, pp. 187–199.

———, "The State, Politics and Religion in Turkey," in Metin Heper and Ahmet Evin (eds.), *State, Democracy and the Military. Turkey in the 1980s*, Berlin/New York: Walter de Gruyter, 1988, pp. 119–136.

———, "Politicization of Islam in a Secular State," in Said Arjomand (ed.), *From Nationalism to Revolutionary Islam*, London: Macmillan, 1984, pp. 119–133.

Tosun, Tanju, "The July 22 Elections: A Chart for the Future of Turkish Politics," *Private View,* Istanbul, No. 12, Autumn 2007.

Transatlantic Trends: Key Findings 2007, Washington, D.C.: German Marshall Fund of the United States, 2007.

"Tüketirken Tükenmek," *Çerçeve*, Nissan 2007. As of February 28, 2008: http://www.musiad.org.tr/yayinlarRaporlar/detay.asp?yayinRapor=46&k=1

Turan, İlter, "Turkey Watch/Politics: Uncertainties of Turkish Politics," *Private View,* Istanbul, No. 12, Autumn 2007.

"Turkey irked by Gaza offensive but not prompted to reverse ties to Israel," *The Probe,* May 30, 2004.

"Turkey Refuses to Back Down on Iran Energy Deal," *Eurasia Daily Monitor,* Vol. 4, No. 157, August 16, 2007.

"Turkey: Religious Minorities Watch Closely as Election Day Approaches," Eurasianet, July 19, 2007. As of March 21, 2008: http://www.eurasianet.org/departments/insight/articles/eav071907a.shtml

"Turkish Constitution" (Turkish), undated. As of February 28, 2008: http://www.tbmm.gov.tr/Anayasa.htm

Turkish Daily News, April 21, 2006.

"Turkish Islamists aim for power," *The Guardian*, November 27, 1995.

"Turkish Police No Nearer to Solving Attempted Ankara Bombing," *Eurasia Daily Monitor*, Vol. 4, Issue 172, September 18, 2007.

"Türkiye'ye daha büyük kötülük yapılamazdı," *Vatan,* January 20, 2007.

"20 milyon mark hangi siyasi partiye gitti?" *Radikal*, November 4, 2006.

Üçer, Murat, "Turkey Watch/Economics: Well Done! But Now What?" *Private View,* Istanbul, No. 12, Autumn 2007.

Ülsever, Cüneyt, "Heart-felt congratulations to the AKP," *Turkish Daily News,* September 5, 2007.

"US critical of Turkey's partnership with Iran," *Turkish Daily News,* April 7, 2007.

"US criticizes Turkey for Iran energy deal," *Turkish Daily News,* September 22–23, 2007.

U.S. Department of State, "Shared Vision and Structured Dialogue to Advance the Turkish-American Strategic Partnership," U.S. Department of State Media Note, July 5, 2006.

———, "Turkey: International Religious Freedom Report 2006." As of March 21, 2008:
http://www.state.gov/g/drl/rls/irf/2006/71413.htm

"US uneasy over Turkey Iran gas deal," *Turkish Daily News,* July 12, 2007.

Verfassungsschutzbericht 2005, Berlin: Bundesministerium des Innern, May 2006. As of February 28, 2008:
www.bmi.bund.de or www.verfassungsschutz.de

Vergin, Nur, "De-Ruralization in Turkey and the Quest for Islamic Recognition," *Private View,* Vol. 1, No. 1, Winter 1996.

"Veteran diplomat, Armenian patriarch lend support to AKP," *Turkish Daily News,* June 5, 2007. As of March 1, 2008:
http://www.turkishdailynews.com.tr/article.php?enewsid=75000

Walker, Joshua W., "'Strategic Depth' and Turkish Foreign Policy," *Insight Turkey,* Vol. 9, No. 3, 2007.

Walker, Martin, and Cengiz Çandar, "The Turkish Dilemma," *The Wilson Quarterly,* Vol. 24, No. 4, Autumn 2000.

Yavuz, Hakan, "Cleansing Islam from the Public Sphere," *Journal of International Affairs,* Vol. 54, No. 1, Fall 2000, pp. 21–42.

———, "Towards an Islamic Liberalism? The Nurcu Movement and Fethullah Gülen," *Middle East Journal,* Vol. 53, No. 4, Autumn 1999.

———, "Political Islam and the Welfare (Refah) Party in Turkey," *Comparative Politics,* Vol. 10, No. 1, October 1997.

Yıldız, Ahmet, "Politico-Religious Discourse of Political Islam in Turkey: The Parties of National Outlook," *The Muslim World,* Vol. 95, April 2003.